ETCHED *in* STONE

ARCHEOLOGICAL DISCOVERIES THAT PROVE THE BIBLE

LISETTE BASSETT-BRODY

FOREWORD BY DR. LON SOLOMON

WND Books

ETCHED *in* STONE

Published by WND Books, Washington, D.C. WND Books is a registered trademark of WorldNetDaily.com, Inc. ("WND")

Book designed by Mark Karis

WND Books are available at special discounts for bulk purchases. WND Books also publishes books in electronic formats. For more information call (541) 474-1776, e-mail orders@wndbooks.com or visit www.wndbooks.com.

Scripture quotations are taken from the Holy Bible, New International Version®, NIV® Copyright ©1973, 1978, 1984, 2011 by Biblica, Inc.® Used by permission. All rights reserved worldwide.

Paperback ISBN: 978-1-944229-79-5
eBook ISBN: 978-1-944229-80-1

Library of Congress Cataloging-in-Publication Data
Names: Bassett-Brody, Lisette, 1965- author.
Title: Archeological discoveries that prove the Bible / Lisette Bassett-Brody
 ; foreword by Dr. Lon Solomon.
Description: Washington, D.C. : WND Books, [2017] | Audience: Grade 9 to 12.
 | Includes bibliographical references and index. |
Identifiers: LCCN 2017018498 (print) | LCCN 2017039296 (ebook) | ISBN
 9781944229801 (e-book) | ISBN 9781944229795 (pbk.) | ISBN 9781944229801
 (ebook)
Subjects: LCSH: Bible--Antiquities--Dictionaries.
Classification: LCC BS622 (ebook) | LCC BS622 .B37 2017 (print) | DDC
 220.093--dc23
LC record available at https://lccn.loc.gov/2017018498

Printed in the United States of America
17 18 19 20 21 22 LBM 9 8 7 6 5 4 3 2 1

I would like to dedicate this book to my mother, Betty R. Bassett. She always inspired me to strive for more and encouraged me to explore new paths. She was a strong, loving, caring person, and I believe it was because of her faithful prayers that I am a follower of Jesus Christ today.

(1923–2000)

CONTENTS

FOREWORD

There has long been the need for a book that collects many of the biblically relevant archaeological discoveries of the past one hundred years in one volume. These discoveries have been manifold and significant. However, when one goes to search for them, they are spread over a cadre of magazines, Internet sites, newspaper articles, and scholarly publications. What has been sorely missing is a single reference book that compiles all this information.

Furthermore, there has been the need for a book that is unburdened by the kind of minutiae that is of interest only to specialists. In this single volume you will find many of the important archaeological discoveries of the last century, catalogued and indexed so that they are easy to locate. You will also find crisp, clear pictures of these finds, collated from the best sources available.

Etched in Stone: Archaeological Discoveries that Prove the Bible offers a clear, concise summary of the biblical events surrounding each artifact. There are also maps at the back to show where in the world the artifact was discovered. Together, they will lead you to realize that the stories of the Bible are neither fictional nor allegorical. Instead, they are historical and factual events that occurred in real time and in real places.

Lisette Bassett-Brody has spent countless hours familiarizing herself with the archaeological data while never losing sight of the needs of her readers. The author's ultimate goal is to increase her readers' confidence in the integrity and veracity of the Bible. As you will see, she has the skill in word and picture to accomplish this goal.

Lisette has heard me say repeatedly the mantra "The more they dig out of the ground, the more the Bible proves to be true." In *Etched in Stone*, she has effectively collated the data that backs up that mantra.

Etched in Stone is a handsome addition to the literature of the Bible and of the land of Israel. It is a valuable book that will be read with profit and pleasure by many.

—DR. LON SOLOMON
SENIOR PASTOR, MCLEAN BIBLE CHURCH, WASHINGTON, D.C., 2017

AUTHOR'S NOTE

"These stones are to be a memorial to the people of Israel forever." (JOSHUA 4:7)

"The Bible is just a fairy tale. There is no physical evidence to support any of it!" This is the kind of fire Christians come under all the time. Where is the physical proof? Isn't there anything out there that corroborates the stories of the Bible? Even Christians ask this question sometimes. Christianity is certainly based on faith, but haven't you ever thought of how wonderful it would be to have something tangible? That is what *Etched in Stone* is all about. This book gives believers something to point to that displays a portion of the *physical* evidence that God, in His wisdom, chose to leave behind.

Etched in Stone is a unique book because it is the only one of its kind on the market today. This biblical archaeology reference book is for laypersons, everyday people like you and me who have an interest in archaeology but do not want to spend hours researching, reading, and trying to understand all of the theology found in most other books.

You may be wondering how I came up with this idea. Well, my story begins in 1983 as a freshman in college. Being so far from home, I felt lost, alone, and without a sense of purpose. Then one night a classmate told me the story of a carpenter from Nazareth whose death on the cross redeems us from sin. As she spoke, I came under the conviction of the Holy Spirit and began to weep tears of joy. I humbly invited Jesus into my heart, and my life was forever changed.

Slowly but surely the Lord continued to teach me and reveal His plan for my life. As a junior, I spent a year in Spain, where I had the opportunity to read and ponder the entire New Testament, an experience that greatly strengthened my faith. Meanwhile, the Lord used me to share the gospel with many others and lead them to Christ.

After graduating from Syracuse University with a BA in modern foreign languages, I married my best friend, David Philip Brody. We moved to Colorado Springs and started a family. Then, in 1995, I realized I needed to expand my understanding of God's Word, so I joined the Community Bible Study program (CBS). I attended CBS for eight years and was a core group leader for three of those years. From there I decided I wanted to go back to school, and in 2013 I graduated summa cum laude from Capital Bible Seminary with an MA in biblical studies.

Over the years I have found time to travel to such places as Japan, Canada, South America, and Europe. But it was in 2000 that I spent two weeks in Israel on a study tour. I could hardly contain myself as I explored the Holy Land and recalled the story of each site according to Scripture. The reports of violence and civil unrest almost dissuaded David and me from going, but God protected us and blessed our journey with tremendous experiences. We visited archaeological digs and toured the Israel Museum, where hundreds of biblical artifacts are on display. It was there that my interest in biblical archaeology began.

Reading and studying the people, places, and things of the Bible is one thing; but seeing them is another. I had no idea of the sheer quantity of biblical artifacts that exists. It is staggering! As a Christian, it was very exciting to finally see so many items that have been written about in the Bible. When I returned stateside, I immediately tried to find a book cataloging the biblical artifacts we had seen. But to my great surprise, there was none. I searched libraries, bookstores, and the Internet—all fruitless. The best I could find were books loaded with *theology* and only a *few* artifacts. I could not help but wonder why these discoveries were not more widely published. Without a doubt, many books catalog biblical artifacts, but they tend to focus on a handful of discoveries and get bogged down in wordy theological discussions. The problem is that most people are not theologians. They just want to know the facts: what's been unearthed, when and where it was found, and what verse of Scripture talks about it. Thus, I decided to compile the information myself because I knew I was not alone in desiring this kind of information. I began in 2005 when I wrote a few articles on archaeology and the Bible for *Bible and Spade* magazine. The articles seemed to be well received, so I moved ahead and started writing my book, *Etched in Stone: Archaeological Discoveries that Prove the Bible.*

Etched in Stone is formatted especially for today's fast-paced, "I want it NOW" society. It is quick and to the point. It has a very straightforward layout that is easy to read, specifically designed to give the reader short but powerful nuggets of information. Christians everywhere will be thrilled to know that there is concrete evidence to support the Bible, and none can dispute the validity of an unearthed artifact. However, this book is not meant to be exhaustive. Any further detailed information you wish to have is easily located on the Internet and in the list of academic sources included at the back of this book.

Etched in Stone is divided into three main sections: "People," "Places," and "Things." Each artifact has two pages dedicated to it. The name of the relic appears at the top of the left-hand page, followed by the verse of scripture that mentions it. In most cases the item will be part of a story, in which case the reference to the entire biblical text is given. A picture of the item follows, and under that is an information box with text indicating the type of item unearthed, the date of discovery, the location where it was discovered, and the name(s) of the archaeologist(s) who led the expedition. Next to "Location" you will also find a reference such as M1, M2, M3, M4, or M5, which will guide you to one of the maps at the back of the book. These maps will give you an idea of where in the world these biblical artifacts were discovered. On the opposite page is a brief summary of the biblical context surrounding the artifact and any pertinent archaeological information. Finally, a quote from a scholarly or secular commentator will affirm the find.

I chose secular commentators for two reasons. First, the general public places greater weight on the words of these commentators. A fundamentalist professor or pastor can talk all day long about King David, for example, but when *U.S. News & World Report* says, "The reference [on the stone] to David was a historical bombshell . . . Now, at last, there was material evidence . . . a clear corroboration of the existence of King David's dynasty and, by implication, of David himself," people take notice. This feature is especially important for those who would like to use the book as a witnessing tool.

The second reason was to reach as wide an audience as possible. I believe people are less likely to dismiss the book out of hand if nonreligious writers have contributed to the work.

Last but not least, I have included a section called "Points of Interest." In this section are items that do not necessarily *prove* the historical actuality of the biblical characters or events named, but do show that there is strong evidence for their historicity.

As you read through the following pages, you may wish to search the Internet for more detailed information on each find. However, do not be surprised or confused by the naysayers. There will always be controversy surrounding anything pertaining to the Bible. It is a book that has been scrutinized more severely than any other document in history, and yet it always passes the test. Nothing within its pages has ever been proven false; rather, false conclusions have been made due to the lack of historical or archaeological information. However, whenever such information surfaces, it has always corroborated the Scriptures. The Dead Sea Scrolls are a perfect example of this. Many had claimed that because the Bible was so old, there had to be countless mistakes between today's version and the original. But in 1947 the oldest known copy of the Scriptures was discovered in various caves in Qumran. What it showed was that the version we have today is entirely accurate and true to its two-thousand-year-old cousin. This was a great victory for Christians and Bible scholars alike who have dedicated their lives to the truths held within and to the belief that the Bible is the inerrant Word of God.

As already mentioned, *Etched in Stone* would also make a great witnessing tool! We Christians no longer have to stare blankly at those who ask for physical evidence and who insist there is nothing concrete to corroborate the Bible. Now you can easily point to some of the thousands of artifacts that have been unearthed.

My desire in compiling this book is to proclaim the truth of God's Word from an archaeological standpoint, and share that truth with the Christian community. Most important, I pray that such a book would touch those who do not profess a faith in Christ and be a source of blessing to them, as well.

I hope you enjoy the information held within these pages. May it touch and bless you in countless ways!

PART I

PEOPLE

AHAZ

2 KINGS 16

In the seventeenth year of Pekah son of Remaliah, Ahaz son of Jotham king of Judah began to reign. Ahaz was twenty years old when he became king, and he reigned in Jerusalem sixteen years. Unlike David his father, he did not do what was right in the eyes of the LORD his God.

(2 KINGS 16:1-2)

ITEM FOUND: Clay seal impression, or bulla, from the eighth century

DISCOVERED: Date unknown

LOCATION: Southern part of the West Bank, Israel (M3)

EXPEDITION: Unknown

Around 1050 BC the people of Israel demanded from God that they be given an earthly king to rule over them because they wanted to be like the other nations around them. God tried to dissuade Israel because He knew the trials, tribulations, and hardships that would follow as a result of man's inability to be just and righteous (see 1 Samuel 8:11–22). However, the people would not listen. So, God appointed Saul as the nation's first earthly king. At this time all twelve tribes of Israel were united. But around 930 BC, the nation split into two groups: the Northern Kingdom, with ten tribes, who kept the name Israel; and the Southern Kingdom, with two tribes, who were known as Judah. Ahaz was a king of the southern tribes of Judah. He ruled from 732 to 716 BC and was not considered righteous because he engaged in idol worship and even sacrificed his son in the fire (see 2 Kings 16:3). Furthermore, when the Southern Kingdom was threatened with a takeover by the Northern Kingdom, Ahaz refused the help God offered him and instead sought help from Assyria (see Isaiah 7). Although God warned Ahaz that Assyria would eventually turn on him, Ahaz stubbornly and foolishly ignored God, and his kingdom suffered the cost.

Archaeology has confirmed the existence of this king. Robert Deutsch, doctor of archaeology and ancient Near Eastern civilizations, from Tel Aviv University and president of the Israel Numismatic Society, confirmed in his book *Messages from the Past* that the seal has been identified. He described it as being "of a high Calligraphic quality" and stated that there is a fingerprint at the edge of the clay daub. "On its left edge, a fingerprint is visible possibly the fingerprint of Ahaz the King of Judah himself." According to Deutsch, expert world authorities such as Frank Moore Cross, of Harvard University, and Andre Lemaire, of the Institut des Recherches Bibliques in Paris, have examined it, and they are all convinced it is genuine.

The inscription reads, "Belonging to Ahaz (son of) Yotam, King of Judah."

AMMONITES

GENESIS 19

So both of Lot's daughters became pregnant by their father. The older daughter had a son, and she named him Moab; he is the father of the Moabites of today. The younger daughter also had a son, and she named him Ben-Ammi; he is the father of the Ammonites of today.

(GENESIS 19:36–38)

ITEM FOUND: Ostraca (pieces of clay pottery with writing on them)

DISCOVERED: 1973

LOCATION: Tell Hesban (biblical Heshbon), Jordan, an ancient tell southwest of Amman, Jordan (M2)

EXPEDITION: Siegfried Horn, 1968–1976

In Genesis 19 Abraham's nephew, Lot, has been visited by two angels of the Lord. He welcomes them into his home, and they inform him that God is going to destroy Sodom, Gomorrah, and the entire plain. The angels then give Lot a chance to warn "anyone else in the city who belongs to [him]," but no one would go with Lot, not even his sons-in-law. As Lot, his wife, and his two daughters run from the city to the relative safety of nearby Zoar, Lot's wife disobeys the instruction of the angels, and when she turns around to view the city's destruction, she turns into a pillar of salt. After the cities and their people have been completely destroyed, Lot and his two daughters move up into the mountains alone. Here the women hatch a perverted idea: since there are no other men around, they should get their father drunk so that they can have sex with him and bear children. Each daughter takes a turn with her father and becomes pregnant. The older daughter names her son Moab, and he becomes the father of the Moabites. The younger daughter has a son and names him Ben-Ammi, and he becomes the father of the Ammonites.

The Ammonites had an extensive biblical history with their cousins, the Israelites. They often teamed up with Israel's enemies, such as the Amalekites, and the Philistines, and repeatedly raided and made war on her. This aggression continued through the time of Saul and King David. But for as prominent a history as the Ammonites had, their land was virtually unknown to Bible scholars until world-renowned American rabbi and archaeologist Nelson Glueck explored the land of Jordan in the 1930s. This was the location where the Ammonites had settled.

Since then, others have brought expeditions to Jordan, and numerous biblical artifacts have been discovered. One such discovery confirmed the existence of this people known as the Ammonites. Larry Herr, doctor of Near Eastern languages and civilizations from Harvard University, described the potsherds that were uncovered:

Found in the fill of the reservoir at Hesban, these two ostraca—potsherds with writing on them—and several others testify to Ammonite survival in their homeland after the Babylonian conquest of Judah in 586 BC. Both bear lists of Ammonite names in the Ammonite language but one is written in the Ammonite script of the mid-sixth century BC, while the other is written in Aramaic script of the late sixth-century BC. In contrast to the closely related paleo-Hebrew script, Ammonite script has an upright stance and simple form. Small changes over time in the letter forms and stance allow experts to date inscriptions with great precision, as in the case of these Ammonite ostraca deciphered by Frank M. Cross.

Today, the capital of Jordan still carries the Ammonite name, that is, Amman.

BELSHAZZAR

DANIEL 5

Then at Belshazzar's command, Daniel was clothed in purple, a gold chain was placed around his neck, and he was proclaimed the third highest ruler in the kingdom.

(DANIEL 5:29)

ITEM FOUND: A clay cylinder from the sixth century BC

DISCOVERED: 1854

LOCATION: Southern Iraq (M4)

EXPEDITION: British consul J. G. Taylor

King Nebuchadnezzar reigned in Babylon circa 605–562 BC. He was the one God used to punish Judah for her idolatry by sending her into exile. When Nebuchadnezzar invaded Jerusalem, he also took the Temple articles, which belonged to the Lord, and placed them in the temple of his god. In the book of Daniel, Belshazzar, Nebuchadnezzar's grandson, is holding a banquet with a thousand of his noblemen, getting drunk. With blatant disregard for the Lord, he orders that the gold and silver goblets, taken from the Jerusalem Temple, be brought in so that he and his guests can drink from them. While engaging in this act of rebellion, he furthers his sin by praising the gods of wood, iron, silver, gold, and stone. Therefore, God tells Belshazzar that his reign is over, and that very night he is killed, effectively ending the Babylonian Empire. Darius the Mede then becomes ruler of the kingdom, effectively beginning the Medo-Persian Empire. Critics scoffed at the story of Belshazzar because they said that no Babylonian records confirmed him. However, in 1854 Babylonian cuneiform records were discovered that did in fact attest to Belshazzar and other details of the time. One such confirmation comes from a clay cylinder discovered in Iraq. In their book, *Lost Treasures of the Bible*, Clyde E. Fant and Mitchell G. Reddish translate a portion of the Babylonian cuneiform concerning Belshazzar:

> As for me, Nabonidus, king of Babylon, save me from sinning against your great godhead and grant me as a present a life of long days, and as for Belshazzar, the eldest son my offspring, instill reverence for your great godhead [in] his heart and may he not commit any cultic mistake, may he be sated with a life of plenitude.

It must be noted here that this clay Nabonidus cylinder states that Nabonidus, who reigned from circa 556 to 539 BC, was Belshazzar's father, while the Scriptures call Nebuchadnezzar Belshazzar's father. It is not uncommon for the Bible to refer to an ancestor as "father." For example, Luke 1:32 calls King David Jesus' "father" whereas we know David was simply his ancestor. This is also a common occurrence in the Middle East even today. Furthermore, it has been confirmed in the cuneiform records that Daniel could have been named "third highest ruler in the kingdom," a fact once contested. Although Nabonidus was the king, he left his son as second in charge while he was away in Teima, in northern Arabia. Therefore, Belshazzar could not have bestowed upon Daniel any higher honor than to be *third* ruler. In his book *Nabonidus and Belshazzar*, Raymond P. Dougherty, who holds a PhD from Yale University, said, "It is an incontrovertible fact that there was a Babylonian prince by the name of Belshazzar; that he acted as co-regent in Babylonia during the absence of his father in Arabia is equally indisputable . . . The scriptural account may be interpreted as excelling because it employs the name Belshazzar, and because it recognizes that a dual rulership existed in the kingdom."

CAIAPHAS

MATTHEW 26-28

Then the chief priests and the elders of the people assembled in the palace of the high priest, whose name was Caiaphas, and they plotted to arrest Jesus in some sly way and kill him. "But not during the Feast," they said, "or there may be a riot among the people." (MATTHEW 26:3-5)

ITEM FOUND: Limestone ossuary

DISCOVERED: 1990

LOCATION: Near Jerusalem, Israel (M2 and M3)

EXPEDITION: Accidental discovery by construction workers

Scripture tells us that Caiaphas was high priest during the time of Pontius Pilate, Roman governor of Judea. He was the leader of the Sadducees, an order of religious Jews like the Pharisees. The Sadducees were an elite group whose interests focused on the written law and Temple ceremonies. They did not expect a messiah to intervene in the affairs of men, nor did they believe in the resurrection. They had a good relationship with the Romans, and they intended to keep it that way.

Because Caiaphas was the high priest, he was also president of the Sanhedrin. The Sanhedrin was made up of seventy men, including the chief priests, scribes, and elders. They functioned as ancient Israel's supreme court. However, their jurisdiction was over Judea only. Although the Sanhedrin were not allowed to put anyone to death, they did have the authority to arrest people and punish them for crimes against their religious laws. This is how Caiaphas was able to arrest Jesus.

With the help of Judas Iscariot, the betrayer, the Sanhedrin sent out a detachment of soldiers and priests to go to the place where Judas led them in order to find and arrest Jesus. During the ensuing trial, with the help of false witnesses, Caiaphas accused Jesus of blasphemy and then sent Him to Pontius Pilate in hopes of securing the death penalty under Roman law. Although Pontius Pilate found no basis for the death penalty, he was afraid of losing the support of the Jewish people, so he did what they wanted and sentenced Jesus to death, that is, death on the cross.

It must be noted here that although it was through the Jewish people, and by the hands of the Romans, that Christ was crucified, it was God's purpose for Him since the beginning of time, and Jesus went willingly. In John 10:17–18 Jesus says, "I lay down my life . . . No one takes it from me." John 3:16 also says, "For God so loved the world that He gave His one and only Son [to be crucified], that whoever believes in Him [and His work on the cross] shall not perish but have eternal life." Every human being has sinned and is in need of a Savior. That's why Jesus died, as a sacrifice for our sins.

Caiaphas was instrumental in the final events of Jesus' life, and it is his ossuary that was discovered. While building a water park south of the Temple Mount, workers accidentally uncovered a hidden burial room from the first century AD. In *U.S. News & World Report*, author and journalist Jeffery Sheler, who holds an MA from Georgetown University, said twelve limestone ossuaries were discovered. One in particular has an inscription on it that reads, "Joseph, son of Caiaphas" while another of the ossuaries has an inscription that simply reads, "Caiaphas." Archaeologists agree that this Caiaphas is the one mentioned in the Bible, and according to Sheler, "[This] find . . . added to the list of Gospel figures whose existence has been verified by archaeology."

CYRUS KING OF PERSIA

EZRA 1-4

In the first year of Cyrus king of Persia, in order to fulfill the word of the LORD spoken by Jeremiah, the LORD moved the heart of Cyrus king of Persia to make a proclamation throughout his realm and to put it in writing: "This is what Cyrus king of Persia says: 'The LORD, the God of heaven, has given me all the kingdoms of the earth and he has appointed me to build a temple for him at Jerusalem in Judah.'" (EZRA 1:1-2)

ITEM FOUND: A nine-inch clay cylinder from the sixth century BC

DISCOVERED: 1879–1882

LOCATION: Babylon, present-day Iraq (M4)

EXPEDITION: Hormuzd Rassam

Cyrus was the king of Persia and founder of the Achaemenid Empire. He reigned from 559 BC to 530 BC. At that time, his empire was the largest one ever to exist because he was able to conquer the Lydian, Median, and Neo-Babylonian empires. His son later conquered Egypt, Nubia, and Cyrenaica. Cyrus respected his conquered subjects' customs and religions, and this is clearly seen in the biblical narrative. In the book of Ezra, Cyrus decrees that all Jews be allowed to return to their homeland and rebuild the Temple in Jerusalem, which was destroyed by the Babylonian king Nebuchadnezzar when he took Judah into captivity in 586 BC. Cyrus also returned the Temple articles belonging to the Lord, which Nebuchadnezzar had placed in the temple of his own god. There were more than five thousand items of silver and gold. Furthermore, Cyrus acknowledged that his power and empire were a blessing from the Lord, and he commanded that those who were willing should provide the exiles with goods, livestock, valuable gifts, and freewill offerings.

In his book *Jerusalem: An Archaeological Biography*, Hershel Shanks, graduate of Harvard Law School, states, "Cyrus' decree is especially believable because a similar edict permitting subject peoples to resettle in their original homes and rebuild ruined sanctuaries has survived in a cuneiform text known as the Cyrus Cylinder."

The *International Bible Encyclopedia* translates a portion of the cylinder thusly: "I am Cyrus, king of the host, the great king, the mighty king, king of Tindir (Babylon), king of the land of Sumeru and Akkadu, king of the four regions, son of Cambyses, the great king, king of the city Ansan, grandson of Cyrus, the great king, king of the city Ansan, great-grandson of Šišpis (*Teispes*), the great king, king of the city Ansan, the all-enduring royal seed whose sovereignty Bel and Nebo love."

The cylinder now resides in the British Museum.

DAVID

2 KINGS 17:1–23

When he [the Lord] tore Israel away from the house of David, they made Jeroboam son of Nebat their king. (2 KINGS 17:21)

ITEM FOUND: Basalt stone slab from the ninth century BC

DISCOVERED: 1993

LOCATION: Tel Dan, Northern Huleh Basin, Israel (M3)

EXPEDITION: Avraham Biran

King David is probably one of the best-known figures from the pages of the Bible. He was the son of Jesse and the youngest of eight brothers. Most would remember him from his victory over Goliath, the Philistine military giant, but there is much more to David than that. He was a shepherd by trade, and when he was still a boy, the prophet Samuel was moved by the Lord to anoint him as Israel's future king. He was a harpist and was best friends with King Saul's son Jonathan (Saul was the first earthly king Israel ever had). However, Saul was jealous of David and tried, on many occasions, to kill him. Moreover, Saul was not faithful to the Lord, so the Lord took the kingdom away from him and gave it to David. David became Israel's second earthly king and had grown to be quite a warrior himself, commanding a powerful army. But he was not without his flaws. David had eight wives and many concubines, which was against the command of Deuteronomy 17:17. He also committed adultery with Bathsheba and ~~murdered~~ SENT her husband to try and cover it up. As punishment, the Lord told David that his household would always be in turmoil, and it was. But overall, David was a good man and a good king. His deepest desire was to serve God completely, in every way. David wrote many of the psalms as he poured out his heart and soul to the Lord, and by grace and mercy was considered "a man after [God's] own heart" (Acts 13:22).

[handwritten margin note: into battle where he was killed by design]

So, did Hebrew scribes invent King David, or was he a historical figure, as the Bible purports? For centuries only the Bible spoke of the very flawed man named David who ruled the united kingdom of Israel. But in 1993 confirmation of his existence came from a most unlikely source. The Aramean king of Damascus, an ancient enemy of Israel, immortalized in stone a military victory over the "House of David." Here's what religion writer Jeffery Sheler had to say about the find:

> The basalt stone was quickly identified as part of a shattered monument from the ninth century BC, apparently commemorating a military victory of the king of Damascus over two ancient

enemies. One foe the fragment identified as the "king of Israel." The other was "the House of David." The reference to David was an historical bombshell. Never before had the familiar name of Judah's ancient warrior king, a central figure of the Hebrew Bible and, according to Christian Scripture, an ancestor of Jesus, been found in the records of antiquity outside the pages of the Bible. . . . [This was] a clear corroboration of the existence of King David's dynasty and, by implication, of David himself.

The stone now resides at the Israel Museum in Jerusalem.

EDOMITES

GENESIS 36; PSALM 137

Remember, Lord, what the Edomites did on the day Jerusalem fell. "Tear it down," they cried, "tear it down to its foundations!" (PSALM 137:7)

ITEM FOUND: Clay cultic vessels

DISCOVERED: 1993

LOCATION: En Hatzeva; Biblical Tamar on the southern border of Judah (M3)

EXPEDITION: Rudolph Cohen and Yigal Yisrael on behalf of the Israel Antiquities Authority

Jacob and Esau were the twin sons of Isaac and Rebekah. When they were still in the womb, God proclaimed that they would become two nations. Thus, the descendants of Jacob were the Israelites, and the descendants of Esau, his older twin brother, were the Edomites, whose territory became known as Edom (M1, M2).

As youths, Jacob was a homebody and Esau was a hunter. One day, when Esau came back from the field hungry and exhausted, he saw that Jacob had cooked some lentil stew. Esau asked for a bowl. Jacob bargained with his brother: a bowl of soup for his brother's birthright. Jacob wanted Esau's birthright because the eldest son of a family received a double portion of the inheritance. He also became head of the household at his father's death, with its rights, privileges, and responsibilities, and he would have been placed in a favored position with God. In this light, it is hard to understand why Esau would have given all that up for a single meal. However, Hebrews 12:16 explains that Esau was "godless."

Over the centuries, the descendants of both Jacob and Esau grew in number and strength. But around 586 BC, in the time of the prophet Obadiah, a word came down from the Lord that Edom would be cut off forever and that there would be no survivors of the house of Esau because they stood by while Israel's enemies conquered them.

Archaeology supports the existence of the Edomites. "The earliest extra-Biblical reference to Edom appears in a late thirteenth century BC Egyptian papyrus, which reports that some Bedouin tribes from Edom stopped at one of Pharaoh Merneptah's forts," wrote the late Dr. Itzaq Beit-Arieh, professor emeritus of Tel Aviv University, in *Biblical Archaeology Review*. "The earliest identification of Edomite pottery was made by the American Rabbi and archaeologist Nelson Glueck, during his excavation of Tell el-Kheleifeh between 1938 and 1940 . . . [However,] the premier investigator of Edomite sites in Edom was the British archaeologist Crystal Bennett. . . . At Umm el-Biyara, Bennett found a seal impression on a jar reading 'Qosgeber King of Edom.' The name of this Edomite King also appears in Assyrian documents of the mid-seventh century BC."

Although the Edomites seem to have descended into a group known as Idumeans during the time of Jesus, Edom ceased to be a state and its people eventually became lost to time, just as God had foretold.

GEDALIAH

JEREMIAH 40-41

When all the Jews in Moab, Ammon, Edom and all the other countries heard that the king of Babylon had left a remnant in Judah and had appointed Gedaliah son of Ahikam, the son of Shaphan, as governor over them, they all came back to the land of Judah, to Gedaliah at Mizpah, from all the countries where they had been scattered. And they harvested an abundance of wine and summer fruit.

(JEREMIAH 40:11-12)

ITEM FOUND: A seal

DISCOVERED: 1935

LOCATION: Lachish, Israel (M2 and M3)

EXPEDITION: Wellcome Archaeology Expedition of England

There are many biblical characters that are known around the world, and the mere mention of their names evokes a full biography of their lives, such as with Adam and Eve, Noah, Moses, and Jesus. Their stories are detailed and tremendously significant for the human race. The Bible has a lot to say about them, and whenever extra-biblical texts or artifacts are discovered, they always support what the Scriptures have to say.

But what about those characters almost no one has heard of? Does the accuracy of the Bible hold up to even the smallest, seemingly insignificant detail of these lesser-known people and accounts? Absolutely, yes! Take Gedaliah, for instance.

During the time of Jeremiah the prophet (ca. 627–560 BC) the people of Judah were very rebellious. Against God's commands, they worshipped idols made by their own hands. They also consulted the stars for direction in their lives, as some might do today with horoscopes. Even their priests and prophets were unfaithful in their spiritual dealings. God gave Judah plenty of warning and plenty of decades to turn from their evil ways, but they refused. So, He sent them to Babylon in captivity, leaving only the poorest of people behind. The king of Babylon, Nebuchadnezzar, destroyed Jerusalem and the Temple, and placed Gedaliah as governor over the poor who remained. Gedaliah assured them that they were safe and that they could plant vineyards and become prosperous while serving the Babylonians. However, Gedaliah's life was cut short when Ishmael, son of Nethanian, murdered him.

Now, more than twenty-five hundred years later, a clay seal has been discovered in Lachish. According to Ernest Wright, doctor of ancient Near Eastern Studies from John Hopkins University, "The inscription in it reads, 'Belonging to Gedaliah, the one who was over the house,' and the reverse side shows the marks of a papyrus roll to which it had been stuck. In other words, it was Gedaliah's personal seal to a letter or official document, which he had just written." Wright also notes that the impression is dated by its archaeological context to the very end of the divided monarchy, indicating that this Gedaliah is the same one whom Nebuchadnezzar made governor of Judah.

Through archaeology, both Gedaliah's existence and his position of authority have been confirmed.

GEMARIAH

JEREMIAH 36

When Micaiah son of Gemariah, the son of Shaphan, heard all the words of the LORD from the scroll, he went down to the secretary's room in the royal palace, where all the officials were sitting: Elishama the secretary, Delaiah son of Shemaiah, Elnathan son of Acbor, Gemariah son of Shaphan, Zedekiah son of Hananiah, and all the other officials. (JEREMIAH 36:11-12)

ITEM FOUND: A clay seal impression, or bulla

DISCOVERED: Summer 1982

LOCATION: Jerusalem, Israel (M2 and M3)

EXPEDITION: Yigal Shiloh, 1978–1985

Most people have heard of Noah, Moses, and King David. These are well-known biblical figures, "great men of the Bible" as many refer to them. Even so, they present a picture of the human condition that we can all identify with: great success one minute, miserable failure the next. But what makes these men so unforget-table is that they had an unshakable faith in their God. Now, many thousands of years later, their tales live on and in their stories we continue to learn valuable life lessons.

But there are hundreds of lesser-known characters in the Bible whose names pop up ever so briefly such that for the most part, we do not even realize we have read their names. Take Gemariah, for example.

Little is known about Gemariah except that he was the son of a man named Shaphan, who held the position of temple secretary. From this information we can derive that he was from a noble family. But the chronicles of the Bible have accurately preserved even characters as obscure as Gemariah. In this case, Gemariah has been identified through archaeology as being a real person. In 1982, in Jerusalem, during an excavation of a building that was destroyed by Nebuchadnezzar in 586 BC, a volunteer accidentally discovered, among the two-thousand-year-old debris, a bulla with Gemariah's name on it, carved in biblical Hebrew, which reads, "Belonging to Gemariah son of Shaphan." This clay seal was, as Christine Temin, former professor at Harvard University and freelance writer for the *Boston Globe*, put it, "thrilling proof that Gemariah was real indeed."

HITTITES

GENESIS 23

Ephron the Hittite was sitting among his people and he replied to Abraham in the hearing of all the Hittites who had come to the gate of his city . . . "Listen to me; I give you the field, and I give you the cave that is in it. I give it to you in the presence of my people. Bury your dead."

(GENESIS 23:10–11)

ITEM FOUND: Text fragment

DISCOVERED: 1906

LOCATION: Hattusha, ancient Hittite capital, present-day Boğazkale, Turkey(M4)

EXPEDITION: Hugo Winckler and Theodore Makridi Bey

The Hittites were a people descended from Ham, the son of Noah. The Hittite territory was located in the land of Canaan (M1). The first Hittite the Bible introduces is Ephron, who sells a plot of land to Abraham in Machpelah, near Mamre, so that he can bury his wife, Sarah, in the cave that was located there. In fact, all three patriarchs (Abraham, Isaac, and Jacob) are buried in this cave, along with their wives. Furthermore, Esau married two Hittite women, and Solomon also had many Hittite wives.

So, are the Hittites a historic people or not? Before the turn of the century, there was no concrete evidence showing that a people referred to in the Bible as the Hittites, existed. This gave Bible critics the opportunity to challenge the idea that this group was real and not a fairy tale. But in 1906, more than thirty thousand text fragments, like the one above, were uncovered in Hattusha, an ancient capital of the Hittites after they invaded the western territory around the eighteenth century BC. "Archaeology has confirmed the presence of a number of fortified Hittite sites . . . strategically located at prominent points across the landscape along the northern frontier," said Billie Jean Collins, doctor of Near Eastern languages and literatures from Yale University.

Today, the University of Pennsylvania offers a degree in Hittite civilization! One can learn about the Hittite economy, which was sustained through their agriculture: mainly wheat, barley, cattle, and sheep. One can also get a look at the governing body, which was dominated by the king, being not only the head of state, but the supreme priest, chief judge, and military commander. Furthermore, the unearthed fragments show that the Hittite language was Indo-European, meaning that it was from the family of English, German, Greek, Latin, Persian, and the languages of India. In fact, Harry Hoffner, doctor of ancient Mediterranean Studies from Brandeis University, and his team have compiled dictionaries of the Hittite language.

With all of these findings, it is safe to say that the Hittite civilization has been forever placed into the pages of history.

JEROBOAM II

2 KINGS 14:23-29

In the fifteenth year of Amaziah son of Joash king of Judah, Jeroboam son of Jehoash king of Israel became king in Samaria, and he reigned forty-one years. He did evil in the eyes of the LORD and did not turn away from any of the sins of Jeroboam son of Nebat, which he had caused Israel to commit. (2 KINGS 14:23-24)

ITEM FOUND: A scaraboid seal of jasper

DISCOVERED: 1903–05

LOCATION: Megiddo, Israel (M3)

EXPEDITION: Gottlieb Schumacher

Jeroboam II (ca. 786–746 BC) was the fourteenth king of Israel. He ruled from Samaria for forty-one years, and his reign was marked by growth and prosperity. He saved his people from the heavy hand of the Syrians and conquered Damascus and Hamath. He also restored the boundaries of Israel from Lebo Hamath to the Sea of the Arabah. Although Jeroboam's reign appears to have been successful, the Bible says "he did evil in the eyes of the LORD" (2 Kings 14:24). Since the time of his forefather Jeroboam I (ca. 928–907 BC), Israel had sinned against the Lord by continuing to worship golden calves, Baals, and Ashtoreths. God had given Israel many warnings that He would not put up with their sin forever, and if they did not change their ways, He would send them into captivity. Israel ignored all of God's warnings for centuries, and finally, in 722 BC, they were taken captive by the Assyrians.

King Jeroboam II has now been confirmed by archaeology. A seal containing his name was found at the royal palace at Samaria. According to David Ussishkin, who holds a PhD from Tel Aviv University, in the book *Scripture and Other Artifacts*, "The seal must have belonged to an official of King Jeroboam of Israel, and since its discovery scholars have generally agreed that Jeroboam should be identified with Jeroboam II (784–748 BC) rather than Jeroboam I (928–907 BC)." The seal measures thirty-seven by twenty-seven by seventeen millimeters. The inscription reads, "(belonging) to Shema, servant of Jeroboam."

KING HEROD
THE GREAT

MATTHEW 2

After Jesus was born in Bethlehem in Judea, during the time of King Herod, Magi from the east came to Jerusalem and asked, "Where is the one who has been born king of the Jews? We saw his star in the east and have come to worship him." (MATTHEW 2:1-2)

ITEM FOUND: Part of a wine jug

DISCOVERED: Summer of 1996

LOCATION: An ancient garbage dump near the synagogue at Masada, Israel (M3)

EXPEDITION: Ehud Netzer, 1995–1997

King Herod the Great ruled Israel from 37 BC to 4 BC. He was the reigning monarch when Jesus was born. He was a harsh ruler and very protective of his kingship. Herod was determined to keep his throne at all costs. He was even known to put those he determined as a threat to death, including several of his sons; his wife Mariamne the Hasmonean and her brother, Aristobulus. Therefore, when he was told that a baby had been born to become the foretold "King of the Jews," he immediately took action. He ordered that all the male children under the age of two in Bethlehem and the surrounding area should be put to death. But God had warned Joseph to take the baby Jesus and His mother, Mary, to Egypt, where they would be safe. Joseph obeyed, and they stayed in Egypt until Herod the Great died. The little family then returned to Israel and settled in Nazareth.

In 1996, archaeologists were rummaging through a garbage heap on Masada, a historically rich, cliff-top fortress that was fortified and furnished by King Herod as a palatial refuge. Located in the western end of the Judean Desert, it boasts not only a breathtaking view of the Dead Sea, but two bath houses, beautiful frescoes, mosaic floors, a synagogue oriented toward Jerusalem, and storage facilities that could hold enough food and water to support an army for many years. It was here that a clay pottery shard with King Herod's name inscribed on it was discovered. This shard came from a two-handled wine jug that was capable of holding about twenty gallons of liquid, and was dated to around 19 BC. In an Associated Press article, archaeologist Ehud Netzer, doctor of archaeology at the Hebrew University of Jerusalem, wrote, "The Latin inscription says either 'Herod, King of Judea' or 'Herod, King of the Jews.'" According to the article, "It was the first time the full title of King Herod, who reigned from 37 BC until his death in 4 BC, had been found in an inscription." But that wasn't the only thing found from King Herod the Great's time. Also uncovered were olive pits, eggshells, pieces of cloth, and basket ware.

KING HEROD AGRIPPA I

ACTS 12

It was about this time that King Herod [Agrippa I] arrested some who belonged to the church, intending to persecute them. He had James, the brother of John, put to death with the sword. When he saw that this pleased the Jews, he proceeded to seize Peter also. This happened during the Feast of Unleavened Bread. (ACTS 12:1-3)

ITEM FOUND: A coin

DISCOVERED: 1945

LOCATION: Talpioth suburb of Jerusalem (M2 and M3)

EXPEDITION: Professor Eliezer L. Sukenik

Many people know Herod the Great from the Bible account of Jesus' birth. He was the one who ordered all the male children two years old and younger in Bethlehem and the surrounding areas to be slaughtered because he was afraid that one of them would one day grow up and replace him as "King of the Jews." He did not understand that the foretold "King" would not be a political figure but one who was concerned with the things of God and heaven.

Herod Agrippa I was the grandson of Herod the Great. He was half-Jewish by his mother, Bernice. Agrippa I was educated in Rome and was so well liked by Caligula and Claudius that they eventually gave him all of Palestine to rule over. To make himself popular with the Jewish community of that day, he gave an air of strictly observing Jewish customs and traditions. He also put the apostle Peter in jail and put the apostle James to death.

Tim Dowley, doctor of church history from the University of Manchester, England, and author of *Discovering the Bible*, said this about the coin of Agrippa I that was unearthed near Jerusalem: "The best preserved and most dramatic of all the coin portraits of New Testament characters is that of Herod Agrippa I (AD 37–44). . . . We have a wonderfully clear coin portrait of Agrippa I, the finest example of which is now shown in the Israel Museum, Jerusalem." The inscription on this coin demonstrates the historical and biblical fact that Agrippa not only habitually glorified himself but he was completely devoted to Rome. The inscription reads, "The great King Agrippa, lover of Caesar."

In the seventh year of his reign, at age fifty-four, this "great" king's life ended abruptly and disgracefully when, according to Acts 12:23, God struck him down, and he was "eaten by worms and died."

KING HEROD AGRIPPA II

ACTS 25-26

A few days later King Agrippa and Bernice arrived at Caesarea to pay their respects to Festus. Since they were spending many days there, Festus discussed Paul's case with the king. He said: "There is a man here whom Felix left as a prisoner. When I went to Jerusalem, the chief priests and elders of the Jews brought charges against him and asked that he be condemned." (ACTS 25:13-15)

ITEM FOUND: Palace ruins

DISCOVERED: 1993

LOCATION: Banias, Israel (M3)

EXPEDITION: Vassilios Tzaferis, Israel Antiquities Authority, 1988–present

The Herodian dynasty started with Herod the Great and ended with Herod Agrippa II. His full name was Marcus Julius Agrippa, and he was the seventh in the family to reign as king. Herod Agrippa I was his father.

Agrippa II ruled over Judea but was very unpopular with his subjects because he did not fully respect the Jewish religion and traditions even though he himself was Jewish. He was very clear that his first allegiance was to Caesar. The Bible tells us that he and his sister Bernice went to Caesarea Maritima to visit the proconsul, Festus. While there, they had an opportunity to hear the apostle

Paul's testimony because he had been imprisoned due to false accusations by the chief priests and Jewish leaders in Jerusalem. After Paul had spoken to Festus and the king, they decided that Paul was innocent, but since Paul had previously appealed to Caesar, he had to go to Rome for another hearing.

In 1993, archaeologists discovered the ruins of a beautiful palace in Banias, Israel. The find belonged to Herod Agrippa II. Herod the Great's son, Philip, chose Banias as his capital and founded the first city here, naming it Caesarea Philippi in honor of himself and Caesar. Later, Herod the Great's grandson, Agrippa II, rebuilt and refurbished the city, ruling over this region from AD 53 to 93. Excavations show that Agrippa's palace was not only large but luxurious as well. It spans almost four acres, and is located at the foot of Mount Hermon near the Banias River.

In his book, *Fifty Major Cities of the Bible*, Dr. John C. H. Laughlin, who holds a PhD from Southern Baptist Theological Seminary, said:

> An incredible complex . . . constructed of large, dressed, limestone blocks . . . has been identified as the royal place of Agrippa II. The palace was constructed in a mirror-like fashion so that the western half is exactly matched by its eastern half. Measuring over four hundred feet wide, from east to west, the palace contained covered passageways, courtyards, a basilica, a fountain and pool, and huge semi-circular guard towers. Evidence of the use of imported marble to decorate the buildings was found in both the debris and in fragments still fastened to the walls with iron nails. On the eastern side of this complex, twelve vaulted rooms, extending more than the length of a football field, were exposed.

Caesarea Philippi disappeared sometime after the Crusades until it was rediscovered in 1805 by Ulrich Seetzen.

NEBUCHADNEZZAR

2 KINGS 24

At that time the officers of Nebuchadnezzar king of Babylon advanced on Jerusalem and laid siege to it, and Nebuchadnezzar himself came up to the city while his officers were besieging it. . . . He made Mattaniah, Jehoiachin's uncle, king in his place and changed his name to Zedekiah." (2 KINGS 24:10, 17)

ITEM FOUND: Palace ruins

DISCOVERED: 1899

LOCATION: Tell Tello, Iraq (M4)

EXPEDITION: Robert Koldewey, 1899–1917

Nebuchadnezzar was king of the Neo-Babylonian Empire. He reigned from circa 605 BC to 562 BC. He is the man who created the famous "Hanging Gardens" for his wife. These gardens became known as one of the Seven Wonders of the Ancient World. In the Bible, God used Nebuchadnezzar to punish Judah for her idolatry and unrepentant behavior. Nebuchadnezzar destroyed the Temple in Jerusalem and brought all the officers, craftsmen, fighting men, and artisans with him to Babylon, leaving behind only the poorest people. He also took everything of value back with him to his country.

In 1899, more than twenty-five hundred years later, a German archaeologist named Robert Koldewey began excavating in Iraq. What he found would make skeptics eat their words. For centuries they had claimed that King Nebuchadnezzar never existed. Now there was insurmountable proof that he was a real person. Koldewey discovered King Nebuchadnezzar's palace complex, which contained not only statues and stelae but countless inscriptions as well. As award-winning journalist Jeffery Sheler, author of *Is the Bible True?* so eloquently put it, "At once, Nebuchadnezzar ceased to be a fictional foil in a supposed Hebrew Mythology; archaeology had affirmed him as a true historical figure." But these were not the only things that confirmed Nebuchadnezzar's existence. The Babylonians themselves left behind detailed records on cuneiform tablets, which were discovered in 1887 at Tell Tello, the ancient Lagash. These records, etched by Israel's ancient enemies, clearly corroborate the words of the Bible:

> In the seventh month (of Nebuchadnezzar-599 BC) in the month Chislev (November/December) the king of Babylon assembled his army, and after he had invaded the land of Hatti (Syria/Palestine) he laid siege to the city of Judah. On the second day of the month of Adara (16th of March) he conquered the city and took the king (Jehoiachin) prisoner. He installed in his place a king (Zedekiah) of his own choice, and after he had received rich tribute, he sent (them) forth to Babylon.

As we can see, the Babylonian account matches almost exactly the one we read in 2 Kings 24.

PHILISTINES

1 SAMUEL 13–14

The Philistines assembled to fight Israel, with three thousand chariots, six thousand charioteers, and soldiers as numerous as the sand on the seashore. They went up and camped at Mikmash, east of Beth Aven. (1 SAMUEL 13:5)

ITEM FOUND: A stone wall relief from the temple of Ramses III at Madinet Habu

DISCOVERED: 1798

LOCATION: Thebes, Egypt (M4)

EXPEDITION: The French Scientific and Artistic Commission

The Philistines were Israel's most notorious enemies. They appeared on the scene circa 1200 BC and were known as Sea People. Their territory was located along the west bank of the country between Gezer and Gaza, near the Mediterranean Sea (M1). The Philistines were descended from Noah's son Ham through his son Mizraim. As cousins to the Babylonians, the Philistines worshipped the gods Dagon and Ashtaroth and had no regard for the Lord. The most infamous Philistine was the mighty military giant Goliath, the one who fought young David and lost (see 1 Samuel 17). Through a number of military exploits and victories, the Israelites were able to expand their territory, although the Philistines always seemed to be a thorn in Israel's side. It was, in fact, the Philistines who killed the first king of Israel, King Saul, and his sons, on Mount Gilboa in northern Israel, and a Philistine woman named Delilah who brought Samson to his ultimate demise when he foolishly revealed the secret to his supernatural strength.

Jeffery Sheler, correspondent for PBS's *Religion & Ethics Newsweekly*, had this to say:

> Modern archaeology has uncovered a wealth of information regarding the Philistine "sea people" thoroughly consistent with their portrayal in the Bible. For example, sources including numerous Egyptian inscriptions indicate that the Philistines most likely originated in the Aegean area, probably on the island of Crete. That fits with biblical passages (Jeremiah 47:4 and Deuteronomy 2:3) linking them with Caphtor, a location most scholars identify with Crete. Additionally, the Bible depicts the Philistines as expert metallurgists, and archaeologists have found material evidence that the Philistines were, indeed, expert metalworkers. . . . Once again, the Bible and archaeology are in agreement.

PONTIUS PILATE

LUKE 23

So Pilate asked Jesus, "Are you the king of the Jews?"

"Yes, it is as you say," Jesus replied.

Then Pilate announced to the chief priests and the crowd, "I find no basis for a charge against this man." (LUKE 23:3-4)

ITEM FOUND: A limestone slab from the first century

DISCOVERED: 1961

LOCATION: In a Roman theater in Caesarea Maritima, Israel (M3)

EXPEDITION: Antonio Frova

When Jesus was about thirty-three, the elders and the chief priests of Israel, known as the Sanhedrin, had Him arrested in the middle of the night. Within a few short hours, they ran Him through a series of unlawful trials. One of these trials took place at the palace of Pontius Pilate, governor of Judea during the reign of the Roman emperor Tiberius Caesar (ca. AD 14–37). When Jesus was questioned, He made no reply of any kind, no matter what false accusations the elders and chief priests hurled at Him. However, Jesus made two very declarative and profound statements. The first was when Pilate asked Him if He was the King of the Jews. To this Jesus replied, "Yes, it is as you say." The second was when the Sanhedrin asked Him if He was the Son of God. Jesus responded, "You are right in saying that I am" (Luke 22:70). Although, in Pontius Pilate's estimation Jesus was odd, he knew that Jesus was not leading any sort of insurrection against Caesar and therefore did not deserve the death penalty. Pilate assessed this treatment of Jesus as motivated by pure jealousy and envy. In an effort to free Jesus, innocent as He was, Pilate offered to release one prisoner in honor of the Passover. But instead of the crowd asking him to release Jesus, the man who had healed their lame, blind, and mute, they asked for the murderer Barabbas to be set free. Pilate did as the crowd demanded and had Jesus crucified.

As usual, Bible critics denied the existence of Pontius Pilate because there was no extra-biblical text confirming him. But in 1961, while excavating the Herodian theater in Caesarea Maritima, workers discovered an inscribed slab of stone with the name Pontius Pilate on it. It was being used as a step within the theater. According to journalist Jeffery Sheler, mentioned previously:

> The discovery of the so-called Pilate Stone has been widely acclaimed as a significant affirmation of biblical history because, in short, it confirms that the man depicted in the Gospels as Judea's Roman governor had precisely the responsibilities and authority that the Gospel writers ascribed to him . . . The inscription reads: "Tiberieum . . . [Pon]tius Pilatus . . . [Praef]ectus Juda[ea]e." According to experts, the complete inscription would have read, "Pontius Pilate, the Prefect of Judea, has dedicated to the people of Caesarea a temple in honor of Tiberius."

Today, the Pilate stone is in the Israel Museum in Jerusalem.

SENNACHERIB

2 KINGS 18–19

In the fourteenth year of King Hezekiah, King Sennacherib of Assyria came up against all the fortified cities of Judah and captured them. . . . One day, while he was worshiping in the temple of his god Nisroch, his sons Adrammelech and Sharezer cut him down with the sword, and they escaped to the land of Ararat. And Esarhaddon his son succeeded him as king. (2 KINGS 19:36-37)

ITEM FOUND: A clay prism

DISCOVERED: 1830

LOCATION: Ancient Nineveh, present-day Kuyunjik, northern Iraq (M4)

EXPEDITION: Colonel Robert Taylor

Sennacherib was the king of Assyria during the time of Hezekiah, king of Judah. One day Sennacherib decided to come against Judah and began to attack her cities and capture them. Hezekiah tried to dissuade Sennacherib and offered to pay him any price he asked. Sennacherib was unreasonable and asked for more than twenty-two thousand pounds of silver and two thousand pounds of gold. Hezekiah paid this price, but in doing so he had to strip the Lord's temple of all its gold and silver as well as empty out the royal treasury. Even so, Sennacherib continued his plan to take over Jerusalem, sending his officials to Hezekiah with a word of warning. This warning included boasting about how he had been victorious over other nations and how no other god had thus far been able to stop him. He even mocked the Lord, claiming that God was powerless to stop him from taking the land and its people. When Hezekiah's men heard this, they tore their clothes as a sign of their indignation against the blasphemy they had just heard. Hezekiah's response was to put on sackcloth and seek the Lord in the temple. He then sent his priests and officials to the prophet Isaiah. Isaiah told them not to worry because the Lord would cut Sennacherib down for his blasphemy. That very night the Lord put 185,000 men in the Assyrian camp to death. Those that survived, along with Sennacherib, withdrew to Nineveh. Shortly thereafter, Sennacherib was worshipping his god, Nisroch, when two of his sons came in and killed him. A third son, Esarhaddon, succeeded him as king. It is interesting to note that Sennacherib boasted that Judah's God could not rescue her from his hand, and yet it was Sennacherib's god who could not rescue him from the Lord!

In 1830, Robert Taylor, British consul general at Baghdad, discovered a clay cylinder in ancient Nineveh, containing the annals of King Sennacherib. According to Ronald Harker, author of *Digging Up the Bible Lands*, the "tablets found in Nineveh confirm the story and are more precise: they say the murder occurred in January 681 BC, in the twenty-third year of the king's reign. Other inscriptions written at the dictation of Esarhaddon give a clue to the patricidal plot. 'Disloyal thoughts inspired my brothers . . . They rebelled. In order to use royal power they killed Sennacherib.'"

The Taylor prism can be seen today in the British Museum.

TIGLATH-PILESER (PUL)

2 KINGS 15:16–22

Then Pul king of Assyria invaded the land, and Menahem gave him a thousand talents of silver to gain his support and strengthen his own hold on the kingdom. Menahem exacted this money from Israel. Every wealthy man had to contribute fifty shekels of silver to be given to the king of Assyria. So the king of Assyria withdrew and stayed in the land no longer. (2 KINGS 15:19–20)

ITEM FOUND: Bas-relief

DISCOVERED: 1853

LOCATION: Nimrud, near present-day Mosul, Iraq (M4)

EXPEDITION: Austen Henry Layard

In His wisdom, after the conquest of Canaan, God had set up a form of government to keep order among His people. This period was known as the time of the judges. The judges each had an area or territory that they monitored, and were sought after by the people to settle disputes and other matters. But the Israelites were not satisfied. They demanded that God allow them to have an earthly king to rule over them, like the pagan nations around them. God warned that an earthly king would demand a tenth of all they owned and the best of their property. He also warned that a king would take their sons into military service and their daughters into domestic service. But the people would not listen. So, God gave them what they wanted, and Saul was anointed as the first king of Israel.

About three hundred years later, a king by the name of Menahem took the throne. The Bible says that Menahem was evil. He began his reign by murdering the sitting king and then attacked those cities that hesitated in subjecting themselves to him. He violently mutilated pregnant women and continued in the sin of Jeroboam— that is, idol worship—established new festivals, and replaced the Levitical priesthood (which God had ordained) with one of his own.

It was during the reign of Menahem that Tiglath-Pileser invaded Israel. Menahem did not feel confident enough to fight against this Assyrian king, so he paid one thousand shekels to ally with him. Menahem reigned for ten years in Samaria, and when he died, his son took over the throne.

In 1853 British archaeologist Austen Henry Layard was excavating a palace in Nimrud, Iraq, where Tigleth-Pileser, also known as Pul, lived. Layard discovered a bas-relief with the name Menahem on it. It showed that Menahem, among other monarchs, was paying tribute to the Assyrian king, just as the Bible relays. In his book, *Archaeology and the Old Testament*, James Pritchard, doctor of Oriental studies from the University of Pennsylvania, said, "[The bas-relief contained] a summary of the campaigns of Tiglath-Pileser III against Israel and mentioned the events which are described by the author of the Book of Kings."

This artifact can be found today in the British Museum.

UZZIAH

2 CHRONICLES 26

Uzziah was sixteen years old when he became king, and he reigned in Jerusalem fifty-two years. His mother's name was Jecoliah; she was from Jerusalem. He did what was right in the eyes of the LORD, just as his father Amaziah had done. He sought God during the days of Zechariah, who instructed him in the fear of God. As long as he sought the LORD, God gave him success.

(2 CHRONICLES 26:3-5)

ITEM FOUND: Funerary inscription

DISCOVERED: 1931

LOCATION: Jerusalem, Israel (M3)

EXPEDITION: Dr. Eleazar Lipa Sukenik of the Hebrew University in Jerusalem

Uzziah was co-regent of the kingdom of Judah from 790 BC to 739 BC. He reigned in the time of the prophet Zechariah. Uzziah listened to the counsel of the prophet and was a good king who obeyed the Lord. Because of this, he was very successful and prosperous. He commanded an army of more than three hundred thousand men and led many effective military operations against the Philistines and Arabs in Gur Baal. He became well-known and very powerful. He rebuilt a number of towns for himself and increased the number of vineyards, cisterns, and towers within his territory. Unfortunately, this king's successes went to his head and he became prideful.

On one particular occasion, Uzziah decided to usurp the God-given authority of the priests by trying to burn incense on the altar in the Temple. This was a great sin. When the priests confronted Uzziah, instead of recognizing his sin and repenting, he began to yell at the priests. In the midst of his rant, Uzziah suddenly found himself inflicted with leprosy and he was immediately ushered out of the Temple. Consequently, Uzziah spent the rest of his days in his own house, separated and alone. He was excluded from the Temple, and his son, Jotham, had to govern the people and take over the responsibilities of the palace. When Uzziah died, he was not allowed to be buried with the kings who had ruled before him because of his leprosy. So, he was buried nearby.

Although this king's story does not seem to end well, it is interesting to note that in the book of Matthew, Uzziah and his son, Jotham, are listed in the genealogy of Jesus. Now, almost three thousand years later, evidence of this ancestor of Jesus has come to light. A bone box was discovered with his name on it. Ernest Wright, doctor of ancient Near Eastern Studies from John Hopkins University and late writer for the *Biblical Archaeologist* journal said:

> Written on [the stone slab] is a remarkable inscription, which reads: :Hither were brought the bones of Uzziah, King of Judah—not to be opened!". . . Linguists tell us that it is written in Aramaic script of the type which was used about the time of Christ. Uzziah, however, was reigning as king of Judah about 775 BC. . . . It would seem that for one reason or another, the traditional grave of Uzziah was cleared, and the bones which were found were gathered up and deposited in a new Mausoleum.

The fact that these bones were so carefully preserved over the centuries shows the amount of respect the people had for this king. Today, the artifact can be seen at the Israel Museum in Jerusalem.

PART II

PLACES

ANTIOCH

ACTS 14

They [Paul and Barnabas] preached the good news in that city and won a large number of disciples. Then they returned to Lystra, Iconium and Antioch, strengthening the disciples and encouraging them to remain true to the faith. (ACTS 14:21-25)

ITEM FOUND: City ruins

DISCOVERED: 1833

LOCATION: Present-day Antakya, Turkey (M4)

EXPEDITION: Francis V. J. Arundell

In the pages of the New Testament, we are introduced to a man named Saul. He was a Jewish Pharisee who was born in Tarsus but raised in Jerusalem. He was highly educated and well versed in the Law. His zeal for God was so strong that he thought he was doing a holy thing when he persecuted the church. In his view, the teachings of Jesus Christ were blasphemous, and he wanted to rid the earth of these teachings. Then one day, while Saul was on his way to Damascus to hunt down more Christians, Jesus met him on the road, changed his heart and his name, and commissioned him as an apostle to the Gentiles, that is, non-Jews.

Saul, now named Paul, went on three missionary journeys to

bring the truth of Christ to the unsaved world. One of the places Paul visited, which was also the starting point of his commission, was the city of Antioch. Antioch was founded in 300 BC by a general of Alexander the Great. It was the main hub for caravans bringing their goods from all parts of the east to the Mediterranean. In Paul's day, Antioch was the Roman Empire's third largest city and was known for its baths, aqueducts, theaters, and temples. Paul and Barnabas preached in the synagogue there, and many Jews and Gentiles put their faith in Christ. Antioch was also the place where followers of Jesus began to be called "Christians" (Acts 11:26).

Antioch's history includes everything from great prosperity in the fourth and fifth centuries to disaster in the twelfth century. Today, most of ancient Antioch is buried under silt and gravel from the Orontes River, but archaeologists have excavated the area, and in his well-known book *The Bible as History*, Werner Keller, doctor of jurisprudence, describes some of the things that have been discovered: "Marvelous reliefs depicted the victories of the emperor Augustus on land, while a frieze with Poseidon, Tritons and dolphins commemorated the naval victory of Augustus at Actium. In the Roman quarters they found the gaming tables where the soldiery whiled away their leisure hours. The archaeologists were looking at the Antioch, so often mentioned, where Paul founded a church on his first missionary journey (Acts 14)."

Excavations of this area have also revealed mosaic floors from the time period of the Roman Empire, which can be seen at the Antakya Archaeological Museum, in modern Antioch.

BETHEL

GENESIS 27-28

Early the next morning Jacob took the stone he had placed under his head and set it up as a pillar and poured oil on top of it. He called that place Bethel, though the city used to be called Luz. (GENESIS 28:18-19)

ITEM FOUND: City ruins

DISCOVERED: 1930s

LOCATION: Ten miles north of Jerusalem (M2)

EXPEDITION: William Foxwell Albright and J. L. Kelso

Bethel, meaning "House of God," is first mentioned in the Scriptures in Genesis 12. It is the location where Abraham first pitched his tent and built an altar to the Lord after leaving his hometown city of Ur. It is also the location from which God had shown Abraham all the Canaanite territories that he and his descendants would inherit. Later, when Abraham's grandson Jacob had to flee the wrath of his twin brother, Esau, he stopped for the night at Bethel and heaven was opened to him. It is from this occasion that we get the reference "Jacob's ladder."

Over the centuries, Bethel continued to be a place where the Israelites sought God and made sacrifices to Him. In time, many of them even settled in Bethel, but by 930 BC the united kingdom of Israel, under David and Solomon, split into two groups: the northern tribe of Israel, ruled by Jeroboam, and the southern tribe of Judah, ruled by Solomon's son, Rehoboam. Because Jeroboam was afraid that his people would go to Jerusalem to worship God and ultimately give their allegiance back to Rehoboam, who ruled from Jerusalem, he decided to build an altar in Bethel where his people could worship. But instead of dedicating it to the Lord, he set up two golden calves, causing the people to commit idolatry. By the time of the prophet Amos, the people of Bethel had become very corrupt. They perverted justice, oppressed the poor, and persecuted God's ministers. God spoke against these behaviors and warned that Bethel would be "reduced to nothing" if they did not repent and change their ways (Amos 5:5).

Bethel became lost during the Middle Ages, somewhere between AD 636 and AD 1098. But around 1930 archaeologists rediscovered it. "The archaeological remains indicate the preeminence of Beth-El in pre-Israelite times and throughout almost the whole Israelite period. Among the finds was a cylinder seal with the images of a god and goddess and the name of the goddess Ashtoreth written in hieroglyphics, showing that Beth-El was undoubtedly an important Canaanite cultic site that was later appropriated by the Israelites for their own use," said Shalom Paul, doctor of Oriental studies from the University of Pennsylvania and professor emeritus of Bible Studies at the Hebrew University of Jerusalem, and William Dever, doctor of biblical theology from Harvard University and distinguished professor of Near Eastern archaeology at Lycoming College in Pennsylvania.

Today, ancient Bethel is called Beitin and is under Palestinian authority. Approximately two thousand people live there.

BETHSAIDA

LUKE 9:1-17

When the apostles returned, they reported to Jesus what they had done. Then he [Jesus] took them with him and they withdrew by themselves to a town called Bethsaida, but the crowds learned about it and followed him. He welcomed them and spoke to them about the kingdom of God, and healed those who needed healing. (LUKE 9:10-11)

ITEM FOUND: City ruins

DISCOVERED: 1838

LOCATION: Two miles north of the Galilee shore (M3)

EXPEDITION: Edward Robinson

How can an entire city be lost: buildings, homes, and streets? Easy. When a city is abandoned, nature takes over and lost it can become. The wind, sun, and rain all play their part in eroding things. Then add a couple of millennia to the mix and what is left is a city buried under a lot of sand and rubble. Bethsaida was just such a city. A small fishing village near the Sea of Galilee, Bethsaida played a significant role in the lives of King David and Jesus. This was the home of several of Jesus' disciples and the location where he performed many of his miracles: healing a blind man, feeding the multitude, and walking on water, to name a few.

So, in 1838 an American minister, Edward Robinson, decided

to search for the lost city using nothing more than the Scriptures and a compass. At that time he identified a mound called et-Tell (the Mound) as the location for Bethsaida. But his claim went unaccepted until 1987 when, with the help of surface surveys and probes, this small village was pinpointed. Archaeologist Rami Arav was the one who officially identified this site, two miles north of the Sea of Galilee, as the lost city. In that same year, the Israeli government formally recognized et-Tell as the site of Bethsaida. In *Biblical Archaeology Review* archaeologists John F. Shroder Jr., Dr. Rami Arav, and Dr. Richard A. Freund said, "This fishing village on the Sea of Galilee simply became lost to history. [Now] not only have we rediscovered the village of Jesus' time, but we are uncovering a rich history going back to the age of King David."

Among the numerous artifacts were an Iron Age palace, a temple, and a Bronze Age city wall. After ten years of excavation, Bethsaida is now open to the public.

BETH SHEMESH

1 SAMUEL 4-7

They [the Philistines] placed the ark of the Lord on the cart and along with it the chest containing the gold rats and the models of the tumors. Then the cows went straight up toward Beth Shemesh, keeping on the road and lowing all the way; they did not turn to the right or to the left. The rulers of the Philistines followed them as far as the border of Beth Shemesh. Now the people of Beth Shemesh were harvesting their wheat in the valley, and when they looked up and saw the ark, they rejoiced at the sight. (1 SAM 6:11-13)

ITEM FOUND: City ruins

DISCOVERED: Mid-nineteenth century

LOCATION: Israel (M2)

EXPEDITION: Edward Robinson and Eli Smith

The Philistine/Israelite border town of Beth Shemesh is mentioned close to two dozen times in the Bible. It was the hometown of the infamous Samson, whose wisdom did not match his strength and whose life ultimately ended in tragedy (see Judges 13:2–16:31). It was the place of an ongoing conflict between the northern tribes of Israel and the southern tribes of Judah, and the town where the Philistines sent the ark of the covenant back to the Israelites to free themselves from the wrath of God (see 1 Samuel 6:1–16).

As with so many sites, the American archaeologist Edward Robinson was the one who first identified the hilltop of Rumeilah as the biblical Beth Shemesh. It is located next to an Arab village called

Ain Shems (Well of the Sun), which in Arabic is "Beth-Shemesh." In *Biblical Archeology Review,* Shlomo Bunimovitz, professor and lecturer of archaeology and ancient Near Eastern civilizations, and Zvi Lederman, doctor of Cultural anthropology from Tel Aviv University, said, "The identification was confirmed by geography." But it wasn't until 1911 that excavations began under a Scotsman named Duncan Mackenzie. Throughout the twentieth century a number of excavations have taken place there. Among the discoveries are a water cistern, a system of fortifications, and several houses with grindstones and clay ovens. Beth Shemesh overlooks the Sorek Valley, located midway between the Mediterranean and Jerusalem.

CAESAREA PHILIPPI

MATTHEW 16

When Jesus came to the region of Caesarea Philippi, he asked his disciples, "Who do people say the Son of Man is?" They replied, "Some say John the Baptist; others say Elijah; and still others, Jeremiah or one of the prophets." "But what about you?' he asked. "Who do you say I am?" Simon Peter answered, "You are the Christ, the Son of the living God." (MATTHEW 16:13–16)

ITEM FOUND: City ruins

DISCOVERED: 1805

LOCATION: 150 miles north of Jerusalem (M2 and M3)

EXPEDITION: John Wilson

Caesarea Philippi was located about twenty-five miles northeast of the Sea of Galilee. It was a place where many false gods were worshipped, such as the Syrian Baal and the Greek god Pan. Herod the Great had even built a marble temple there in honor of the godhead of Caesar. It was in this location, overlooking a fertile valley, that Jesus asked His disciples who they thought He was. Placing Himself against the false religions of that day, He seemed to be asking them to critically compare what they knew of the various gods with whom He was and what He offered. In ten short words Peter accurately confessed the true identity of Jesus: "You are the Christ, the Son of the living God." Jesus then commended Peter for his understanding even though it was God the Father who had revealed it to him. Caesarea Philippi was also where Jesus told the disciples what was to happen to Him. That is, He was to be tortured and killed by the chief priests, elders, and teachers of the Law, but in three days He would rise again. This would be the ultimate proof of His divinity.

Caesarea Philippi may have been destroyed by an earthquake in the fourth century, but today excavations have unearthed many architectural finds. This Roman city housed a Roman bath, a theater, stone sculptures, and shops. There was even a palace that stretched over two hundred yards, with artwork, mosaic floors, and a fountain.

In the Austin *American-Statesman*, Mary Rourke, who holds an MA in religion and the arts from Yale University, said:

> If you want to learn something new about the Bible, you have to dig it up. John Wilson, an archaeologist and Scripture scholar, decided that much 20 years ago. That led him to excavate Caesarea Philippi, an abandoned city in northern Israel near the Syrian border. Romans built it in the first century; the Gospel writers include it among the places Jesus visited. It is probably best known as the city set in the foothills of Mount Hermon, where Jesus revealed his divine nature to his apostles.

CANAAN

GENESIS 10

Later the Canaanite clans scattered and the borders of Canaan reached from Sidon toward Gerar as far as Gaza, and then toward Sodom, Gomorrah, Admah and Zeboiim, as far as Lasha. (GENESIS 10:18-19)

ITEM FOUND: A stele

DISCOVERED: 1896

LOCATION: Thebes, Egypt (M4)

EXPEDITION: Flinders Petrie

Adam and Eve are the mother and father of humankind. But after the Flood the only people left were Noah, his wife, their three sons (Shem, Ham, and Japheth) and their wives. This means the entire human race came from one of Noah's three sons (M5).

The next logical question, then, is, "If Noah's Ark landed on Mount Ararat in Turkey, how did people end up in other parts of the world?" To answer this question one must look at the eleventh chapter of Genesis. Here the Lord says that the whole world had one language and one common speech. As Noah's descendants increased, they began moving eastward and settled in Shinar (M5). At a certain point the people decided they would build a city and a tower high enough to reach heaven, but the Lord did not approve. Therefore, he scattered the people over the earth and confused their language. One group, which descended from Noah through his son Ham, was the Canaanites. Ham's son Canaan was the father of the Canaanites, and they were accursed of God. This is because Ham was sexually depraved, and the Canaanites were no better. They engaged in vile behavior, such as incest, bestiality, homosexuality, adultery, child sacrifice, and idolatry, all forbidden by God. It is no wonder that when God took the Israelites out of Egypt under Moses, He commanded them to destroy everything in the land of Canaan (M1): all the carved images, idols, and high places, as well as all the people and animals. In His mercy God had been patient over many centuries, giving the Canaanites numerous warnings of impending doom if they did not repent and turn from their ways. But the people ignored and mocked God and ultimately received the punishment they deserved.

The Canaanites have now been confirmed and immortalized not only in the pages of the Bible but in extra-biblical texts as well. A ten-foot-tall black granite stele has been discovered that depicts the gods Amun-Re, Mut, and Khonsu and mentions the victories that the Egyptian king Merneptah won over various peoples, including Canaan. In his book *Recent Discoveries in Bible Lands*, William F. Albright, doctor of literature and philosophy in Semitic languages from Johns Hopkins University, translated a portion of the text: "Canaan is despoiled, with every evil [treatment]: Ashkelon has been captured, Gezer has been taken, Yanoam has been destroyed; Israel has been laid waste, it has no offspring [lit. Seed]; Khuru [Palestine-Syria] has become a widow for Egypt."

Presently, the stele is located in the Cairo Museum.

CAPERNAUM

MARK 1

They went to Capernaum, and when the Sabbath came, Jesus went into the synagogue and began to teach. The people were amazed at his teaching, because he taught them as one who had authority, not as the teachers of the law. (MARK 1:21-22)

ITEM FOUND: City ruins

DISCOVERED: 1838

LOCATION: Galilee, Israel (M3)

EXPEDITION: American archaeologist Edward Robinson

In the time of Jesus, Capernaum was a fishing village located on the northern shore of the Sea of Galilee. Although Jesus grew up in Nazareth, He chose Capernaum as His home base during His three-and-a-half-year ministry. It was from this town that Jesus chose four of His disciples: Simon Peter, his brother Andrew, James, and his brother John. He also spent much time preaching the good news, teaching in the synagogues, healing the sick, and exorcising demons. Furthermore, Jesus performed a number of other miracles in Capernaum. He healed the apostle Peter's mother-in-law of a fever and a centurion's paralyzed servant who lay suffering. He also taught His disciples a lesson in faith, trust, and the power of God when He calmed a storm.

Jesus used every opportunity to explain who He was. When four men came with their paralytic friend to be healed by Jesus, they showed tremendous faith by lowering him on a mat, down through the roof, and placing him directly in front of Jesus. They had to do it this way because there were so many people at the house there was no way to get in through the door. When Jesus saw what they had done, He told the paralytic that because of his faith his sins were forgiven. However, only God has the authority to forgive sins, and so, to prove that He was in fact God, Jesus told the paralytic to get up and walk home, and in the sight of all, the healed man did so. Jesus did this so that everyone there could see with their own eyes that Jesus was who He claimed to be and that the only way to eternal life was through Him. Jesus warned the people of Capernaum against their unbelief and unrepentant hearts. He warned that if they did not change their ways, their fate would be worse than that of Sodom and Gomorrah. Ultimately, by the end of the first century, the town of Capernaum was destroyed and remained in ruins for centuries.

In 1838, the town of Capernaum was rediscovered. Here is what renowned religion writer Jeffery Sheler had to say in his book, *Is the Bible True?*

> One ancient town whose authentic connections to Jesus are widely acknowledged today is Capernaum, an impressive archaeological complex known as Tell Hum on the northwest shore of the Sea of Galilee . . . It was identified as the city where the gospels say Jesus lived for a time. . . . Further exploration beginning in the 1960s revealed . . . the ruins of . . . a first century synagogue . . . almost certainly the one visited by Jesus.

Today, Capernaum is open to the public, and there are tours of the synagogue, the ruins of homes, and Peter's house.

EN GEDI

1 SAMUEL 24

After Saul returned from pursuing the Philistines, he was told, "David is in the Desert of En Gedi." So Saul took three thousand chosen men from all Israel and set out to look for David and his men near the Crags of the Wild Goats." (1 SAMUEL 24:1-2)

ITEM FOUND: City ruins

DISCOVERED: 1961

LOCATION: Ein Gedi, Israel (M3)

EXPEDITION: Benjamin Mazar, on behalf of the Hebrew University and the Israel Exploration Society.

En Gedi (also known as Ein Gedi) is an oasis near the Dead Sea, on the eastern border of the Judean Desert. Its elevation ranges from the lowest point on earth to about 650 feet above sea level. This territory was given to the tribe of Judah when the Israelites left the desert and moved into the land of Canaan. Centuries later, when David was fleeing from King Saul, he lived in the strongholds of En Gedi. Although this desert area is very dry and hot, there are four freshwater springs that run through it year-round. This is what has made it possible for Judah, David, and people today to settle in the area.

According to the Israeli Foreign Ministry:

The first permanent settlement [in En Gedi] was built on the low hill, Tel Goren, at the end of the monarchic period (second half of the 7th century BCE). The houses of the small village were built close together on terraces; each consisted of two rooms and a courtyard. In them were large clay vats for the storage of drinking water or liquids made from special plants growing in the area. Royal seal impressions and others bearing personal names, as well as a hoard of silver pieces were found in the ruins of the village, indicating wealth and economic importance.

Today, En Gedi is home to a nature reserve and was declared a national park in 2002. Ibex, desert leopards, and birds are among the vast variety of animals and plants that can be found here. En Gedi is open to the public and has many things to see and do, such as walking trails and natural pools in which to take a swim. There are even ancient ruins to explore, such as a newly restored synagogue and a Chalcolithic temple. Modern-day buildings are also found, including a kibbutz and a youth hostel.

GATH

1 CHRONICLES 17–18

In the course of time, David defeated the Philistines and subdued them, and he took Gath and its surrounding villages from the control of the Philistines. (1 CHRONICLES 18:1)

ITEM FOUND: City ruins

DISCOVERED: 1996

LOCATION: Tel es-Safi, central Israel, on the southern bank of the Elah valley (M2 and M3)

EXPEDITION: Aren Maeir, professor at Bar-Ilan University and director of the Tell es-Safi/Gath Archaeological Project

In ancient times, Gath was one of five Philistine cities, along with Ekron, Gaza, Ashkelon, and Ashdod. In the eleventh century BC, Israel went to war with the Philistines to free herself from harsh servitude. Unfortunately, Israel lost four thousand men on the first day. Instead of turning from their sin and inquiring of the Lord what they should do next, the Israelites decided to bring the ark of the covenant into battle, supposing that God, who was "enthroned between the cherubim," would be forced to help them (see 1 Samuel 4:4; 2 Samuel 6:2; among others). This plan backfired because no one can force God's hand. Furthermore, the Israelites were putting their faith in an object rather than in their God. Israel ended up losing thirty-thousand more soldiers, and the Philistines captured the ark. They brought it to the city of Ashdod, but the Lord caused the people to break out in tumors. So, they sent the ark to the Philistine city of Gath, and when the people there broke out with tumors, they sent the ark to Ekron. However, the Philistines refused to allow the ark to enter because they were afraid the Lord would kill them all. Finally, after seven months, they decided to send the ark back to the Israelites so the Lord would heal them of their afflictions.

Gath is also noted as the hometown of the infamous giant Goliath, who fought the boy David and lost. When David became a man, the king of Gath, Achish, allowed David to serve him for sixteen months while he was running for his life from a very jealous King Saul. When Saul eventually died in a battle with the Philistines, David eulogized him with a song that he required all his men to learn. It stated: "Tell it not in Gath [that Saul is dead], proclaim it not in the streets of Ashkelon, lest the daughters of the Philistines be glad, lest the daughters of the uncircumcised rejoice." Gath did not boast for long though. Approximately two hundred years later a Judean king named Uzziah conquered the Philistines and took over a number of their cities, including Gath.

In 1996, Aren Maeir and his team began digging atop a tell, Tell es-Safi, in central Israel between Jerusalem and Ashkelon, hoping to find the Philistine city of Gath. Almost immediately, they uncovered the foundations of buildings. In 2001, in the *Jerusalem Post*, former managing editor Calev Ben-David said, "In the past five years, Maeir and his team have . . . discovered a rich trove of Philistine artifacts—richly decorated pottery, jewelry, and cultic items. These items, and the extent of the remains found at Tel es-Safi, offer what Maeir calls '99 percent proof' that the site was ancient Gath." Today, Gath remains an archaeological site.

GIBEAH

JUDGES 19-20

That evening an old man from the hill country of Ephraim, who was living in Gibeah (the men of the place were Benjamites), came in from his work in the fields. When he looked and saw the traveler in the city square, the old man asked, "Where are you going? Where did you come from?" (JUDGES 19:16-17)

ITEM FOUND: City ruins

DISCOVERED: 1922–1923

LOCATION: Tell el-Ful, three miles north of Jerusalem (M2 and M3)

EXPEDITION: William Foxwell Albright, director of the American School of Oriental Research in Jerusalem

When the Israelites left the desert in which they had been wandering for forty years, God instructed them to take the land of Canaan as their inheritance. Joshua led the people into battle and successfully took over much of the land and its territories. Afterward, Joshua cast lots before the Lord to see which tribes would inherit which towns, villages, and cities (see Joshua 18:8–10). Gibeah was a city a few miles from Jerusalem that was given to the tribe of Benjamin (see Joshua 18:28). Later, in the book of Judges, we are given a glimpse of the moral and spiritual decay of the Benjamites living there.

Judges tells us of a Levite who decided to travel from Bethlehem to "the house of the LORD" (19:18). At that time, the Bible says, there was no king in Israel. With the Levite were his servant and his concubine. Since it was a long journey and night had fallen, he decided to stop at Gibeah. An old man who was living there hospitably took them into his home.

Suddenly, the house was surrounded by wicked men who demanded that the Levite be handed over to them so they could have sex with him. The old man refused, and the Levite gave them his concubine instead. Throughout the night she was raped and abused until she died. The next day, in feigned indignation, the Levite cut her into twelve pieces, sending each piece into all the regions of Israel. Together, the Israelites came against the Benjamites and demanded that the evildoers be handed over so that they could put them to death. The Benjamites refused, and a war began between the two groups. Israel asked the Lord what to do, and He confirmed that they should keep fighting because they would win. So, on the third day, the Israelites ambushed the Benjamites and put them all to the sword, including everyone in their towns and even their animals. Lastly, they set their towns on fire.

Centuries later, archaeologist William F. Albright discovered Gibeah when he decided to dig at a mound he felt was appropriate in size and location. In their book, *Treasures from the Dust*, Azriel Eisenberg, doctor of Hebrew letters from Jewish Theological Seminary, and Dov Peretz Elkins, doctor of ministry in counseling and humanistic education from Colgate Rochester Divinity School, said:

> The investigation showed that the site was destroyed in the twelfth century, during the period of the Judges. It was in this very period, during an intertribal war among the Israelites, that "the whole city went up in smoke to heaven," according to the Bible (see Judges 20:40). This was no doubt the event that caused the layer of ashes found by Albright on the twelfth century B.C. occupation level at Gibeah—a striking confirmation of biblical history.

HAZOR

JOSHUA 8-11

At that time Joshua turned back and captured Hazor and put its king to the sword. (Hazor had been the head of all these kingdoms.) Everyone in it they put to the sword. They totally destroyed them, not sparing anything that breathed, and he burned up Hazor itself. (JOSHUA 11:10-11)

ITEM FOUND: Clay tablets

DISCOVERED: 1996

LOCATION: The royal palace of Hazor, ten miles north of the Sea of Galilee, Israel (M3)

EXPEDITION: Hebrew University, joined by the Complutense University of Madrid, resumed in 1990 under Amnon Ben-Tor.

When Joshua and the Israelites left the desert and entered Canaan, their main goal was to take over the land and possess it as the Lord had commanded. Joshua went throughout the country, attacking their royal cities and putting everyone to death, including their kings. One such city was Hazor. Jabin, king of Hazor, was the head of all the kingdoms. So, when he heard about Joshua's conquests, he quickly called together all of the kings of the land, and they came with their armies, "as numerous as the sand on the seashore" (Joshua 11:4). However, these armies were no match for the Lord, and Joshua defeated every single one.

Located in Upper Galilee, Hazor is the largest archaeological site in northern Israel. Here is what Ross Dunn, late foreign correspondent to the *Times of London,* had to say:

> By the time of Abraham . . . the city, which was on the main trade route between Egypt and Babylonia, had become a center for commerce in tin, silver, gold and precious stones. One of the four tablets [discovered] displays multiplication tables. Another details a civil dispute between city residents and a third carries a list of goods sent from Hazor to Mari, another important Canaanite city in Babylonia. The list includes the first mention of the name Hazor to be found in an inscription at the site, thereby confirming the biblical story of the city's existence.

Excavations originally began in the 1950s, and in 2005, UNESCO named Hazor a World Heritage Site along with other biblical tells, such as Megiddo and Beersheba.

HEBRON

GENESIS 23

So Ephron's field in Machpelah near Mamre—both the field and the cave in it, and all the trees within the borders of the field—was deeded to Abraham as his property in the presence of all the Hittites who had come to the gate of the city. Afterward Abraham buried his wife Sarah in the cave in the field of Machpelah near Mamre (which is at Hebron) in the land of Canaan. So the field and the cave in it were deeded to Abraham by the Hittites as a burial site. (GENESIS 23:17-20)

ITEM FOUND: Jagged stone walls and ramparts

DISCOVERED: 1999

LOCATION: Hebron, Israel (M3)

EXPEDITION: Emanuel Eisenberg of the Israel Antiquities Authority

The city of Hebron has truly played a significant role in the history of God's people. Abraham, one of the best-known figures of the Bible, was the first of this group to settle here. When his wife Sarah was 127 years old, she died, and Abraham needed a place to bury her. So, he bought a field and a cave from a man named Ephron for four hundred shekels (ten pounds) of silver. The Bible says that not only was Sarah buried here, but Jacob, his wives, a number of his sons, and Abraham himself were also laid to rest in this cave in Hebron.

More than 460 years later, Moses led the Israelites out of slavery in Egypt. God instructed the people to conquer the land of Canaan and take it as their inheritance. Moses sent out spies to gather information. The spies went to Hebron and found that it was indeed "flowing with milk and honey," as God had promised (see Exodus 3:8, 17; 13:5, among others). However, the Israelites were afraid of the people who already inhabited the land, and they refused to enter Canaan. Only Joshua and Caleb were willing to obey God. So God subjected His people to wander the desert for forty years until the disobedient generation had passed away. When the Israelites finally stepped out in faith, with Joshua and Caleb leading, they took possession of most of the territory and divided it among the twelve tribes of Israel (M2). Within the territory that the tribe of Judah received, the descendants of Aaron were allotted the city of Hebron and its pasturelands, but the fields and the villages around Hebron were allotted to Caleb and his descendants. Centuries later, God sent David to settle in Hebron, where he was anointed king. He ruled from Hebron for seven and a half years and had several sons born to him there.

In 1999, homes were to be built at the edge of Tel Rumeida. However, the law in Israel requires that before any construction, a "rescue dig" must be performed. This is to ensure that no ancient artifacts as yet unearthed would be inadvertently destroyed. It was during one of these rescue digs that the city wall of ancient Hebron was discovered. In the *Houston Chronicle*, former Jerusalem correspondent Deborah Horan quoted archaeologist Emanuel Eisenberg as saying, "This is the biblical city, the ancient site of Hebron. And this," pointing to the discovery, "is more or less the wall that Abraham could have seen when he dealt with the ruler of this place to buy the burial ground for his family, where the Tomb of the Patriarchs is today."

"The outer wall of the city dates to 1600 B.C. and is less than one mile from the site where both Jews and Muslims believe that Sarah, Abraham, and other biblical figures are buried," said Horan.

MEGIDDO

1 KINGS 9:15–11:6

Here is the account of the forced labor King Solomon conscripted to build the LORD's temple, his own palace, the supporting terraces, the wall of Jerusalem, and Hazor, Megiddo and Gezer. (1 KINGS 9:15)

ITEM FOUND: City ruins and a water tunnel

DISCOVERED: 1925–39

LOCATION: Megiddo, Israel (M3)

EXPEDITION: The Oriental Institute of the University of Chicago, financed by John D. Rockefeller Jr.

The first time the Scriptures introduce us to Megiddo is when Joshua and the Israelites finally stopped wandering in the desert (ca. 1446 BC) and moved into the land of Canaan to conquer the people living there. There were thirty-one royal cities in this area, each with its own king, and Megiddo was one of these cities listed in the book of Joshua. It was located in the territory that was given to the tribe of Issachar (M2). Unfortunately, the Israelites did not obey the Lord when He commanded them to completely destroy the people living in Canaan (the Lord did not want the Israelites to learn to worship the false gods of the Canaanites). Instead, they conquered the land and put the survivors to forced labor, which was in direct violation of what they were told to do. Over the next few centuries, the Israelites did, in fact, begin worshipping false gods and intermarrying with the people of Canaan. Furthermore, the Israelites were always at odds with the Canaanites and were often oppressed by them. By 1050 BC, Israel had demanded that God give them an earthly king to rule over them and lead them into battle when necessary. So God appointed Saul as Israel's first king. Next came David, and in 970 BC, his son Solomon succeeded him. Solomon's forty-year reign was marked with peace and prosperity. According to 1 Kings 9:15–19 Solomon built the Temple in Jerusalem as well as his own palace, and built up his store cities, including the towns for his horses and chariots. One of the many projects Solomon undertook was fortifying the city of Megiddo.

In their book, *Biblical Archaeology,* Shalom Paul and William Dever, mentioned previously, state:

> Clearly, when Solomon rebuilt Megiddo, with its large palaces, casemate walls, and massive gate, he also made sure of the town's water supply in times of danger. Thus the terse biblical statement that Solomon built Megiddo has been greatly amplified by archaeological excavations which have shown his activities to have covered the three essential features of the ancient city: the buildings, the fortifications, and the water supply.

Today many of the artifacts that were discovered, such as jewelry and ivory carvings, are housed at the Rockefeller Museum in Jerusalem and the Oriental Institute of Chicago.

NAZARETH

LUKE 1:26-56

In the sixth month, God sent the angel Gabriel to Nazareth, a town in Galilee, to a virgin pledged to be married to a man named Joseph, a descendant of David. The virgin's name was Mary. The angel went to her and said, "Greetings, you who are highly favored! The Lord is with you."

(LUKE 1:26-28)

ITEM FOUND: An inscription

DISCOVERED: 1962

LOCATION: Caesarea Maritima, Israel (M3)

EXPEDITION: Professor Nahman Avigad from Hebrew University

The Bible tells us that Jesus grew up in the small town of Nazareth but was born in Bethlehem. It was in Nazareth that Jesus' mother, Mary, first received the news from the angel Gabriel that she had been chosen to give birth to "the Son of the Most High" (Luke 1:32, 35). Although we don't know much about the Nazareth of Jesus' day, Scripture gives us a picture of the city that is anything but flattering. When Nathanael, who was to become one of Jesus' disciples, was beseeched by Philip, also a future disciple, to come see the "the One Moses wrote about in the Law"—that is, Jesus of Nazareth, the promised Messiah—he responded with surprise, saying, "Nazareth! Can anything good come from there?" (John 1:45–46). Perhaps this was because Nazareth was not considered to be a town where prophecy was expected to be fulfilled. Furthermore, we can glean from other verses what may have been part of the problem: they knew Jesus as one of their own and had a hard time seeing Him as the promised Messiah. The apostle Mark tells us that Jesus could not perform many miracles there because the people did not believe in Him. They questioned His authority, and saw Him as not much more than a carpenter (See Mark 6:1–6). In fact, while in Nazareth, after Jesus entered the synagogue and read from the Scriptures, He hinted to the people that because of their unbelief God's message would not have as much of an impact on them. They needed to open their hearts to God. Instead of repenting, the townspeople tried to kill Jesus by throwing Him off a cliff, but He escaped (see Luke 4:16–30).

Today, Nazareth is the largest city in the Northern District of Israel. Located sixteen miles from the Sea of Galilee and overlooking the Jezreel Valley, Nazareth enjoys a mild climate year-round. There are more than seventy thousand Jews, Christians, and Muslims living in Nazareth at present, but in Jesus' day it was a small town not worthy of mention in the Old Testament or any extra-biblical texts. According to the editors of Time-Life Books, "Such an omission led some scholars to question its existence in New Testament times at all. But in 1962, archaeologists found an inscription naming

Nazareth as one of the towns where members of Judaism's priestly classes settled after the destruction of Jerusalem in AD 135." Dated to circa AD 300, this piece of archaeological evidence was discovered on a marble fragment in a synagogue in Caesarea Maritima on the Mediterranean Coast of Israel.

NINEVEH

BOOK OF JONAH

The word of the Lord came to Jonah son of Amittai. "Go to the great city of Nineveh and preach against it, because its wickedness has come up before me." . . . Now Nineveh was a very important city—a visit required three days.

(JONAH 1:1-2; 3:3)

ITEM FOUND: City ruins and tablets

DISCOVERED: 1846

LOCATION: Nineveh, near Mosul in northern Iraq (M4)

EXPEDITION: Austen Henry Layard

Noah's son Ham had a grandson named Nimrod. Nimrod built the city of Nineveh, which became a principal capital of Assyria. It was a very beautiful, wealthy city with a great number of inhabitants, and its power and dominion were supreme at that time. Unfortunately, the Assyrians were brutal people. They lived for war and violence, and were notorious for their cruelty. Around 760 BC their wickedness had grown to such a degree that the Bible says they were on the verge of being destroyed by the Lord. However, in His mercy God sent them a warning through the prophet Jonah. The Ninevites believed God's message, and they repented, fasted, and turned from their evil ways. Because Nineveh responded appropriately, God spared them.

Fewer than fifty years later, the Assyrians were back to their old ways. King Sennacherib marched against the Judean king Hezekiah and all of God's people. He mocked God and set himself above Him. In response, God put 185,000 Assyrian military men to death, effectively protecting His own. At the sight of his dead army, Sennacherib returned to his capital city of Nineveh and was murdered by two of his sons while worshipping his false god, Nisroch (see also "Sennacherib").

Sennacherib's son Esarhaddon took the throne, and Assyria continued to oppress Judah. But around 660 BC, the prophet Nahum delivered a prophecy, once again of destruction, to Nineveh, stating that because they continued to oppose God, plot evil, torment surrounding nations, and oppress His people, they would suffer permanent destruction. Then, in 612 BC the Chaldeans and the Medes attacked and burned Nineveh, and it never regained its former glory or prominence again.

In his book, *Royal Cities of Assyria*, Gordon G. Garner, who holds an MDiv from Melbourne College of Divinity in Australia, wrote:

Today Nineveh is represented by two mounds, Kuyunjik and Nebi Yunus, located within the embankments concealing the remains of the defensive walls . . . Practically all we know about Nineveh and its remains comes from this site. Here periodical investigations over a century have uncovered much of the Assyrian treasures that now rest in the British Museum . . . This includes the famous Lion Hunt Reliefs . . . showing the head of the king of Elam hanging from a tree whilst the Assyrian king and queen celebrate a victory feast below.

SAMARIA

1 KINGS 16:23-28

In the thirty-first year of Asa king of Judah, Omri became king of Israel, and he reigned twelve years, six of them in Tirzah. He bought the hill of Samaria from Shemer for two talents of silver and built a city on the hill, calling it Samaria, after Shemer, the name of the former owner of the hill. (1 KINGS 16:23-24)

ITEM FOUND: City ruins

DISCOVERED: 1908–10

LOCATION: Samaria, central mountains of Israel (M3)

EXPEDITION: George A. Reisner through Harvard University's Committee on Exploration in the Orient

Most people are probably familiar with the phrase *being a good Samaritan.* But do they realize it comes from a parable that Jesus told (see Luke 10:29–37)?

Leviticus 19:18 says that we are to love our neighbor as ourselves because this sums up the entire Law (see Galatians 5:14). Jesus' audience wanted to know who was considered a "neighbor." So Jesus told them a story about a man who had been robbed, beaten, and left for dead. Two men passed by: first a priest, then a Levite, but they did nothing to help. Finally, a Samaritan walked by and felt sorry for the man. So he picked him up and took care of his needs. Jesus then asked, "Which was the man's neighbor?" They answered that the one who took pity on the injured man was his neighbor, and Jesus agreed, saying, "Go and do likewise." The point is that we are all neighbors because we are all brothers and sisters from the same human race, and we all need to be good to one another.

Jesus was quite purposeful in picking a Samaritan to be the hero of this parable. This is because the Jews despised Samaritans. In 722 BC the Assyrian king Sargon II conquered the city of Samaria and brought its people into captivity because they had continuously sinned against the Lord with their idol worship. Sargon II then took people from "Babylon, Cuthah, Avva, Hamath and Sepharvaim and settled them in the towns of Samaria to replace the Israelites" (2 Kings 17:24–25). However, these new inhabitants, although they were taught how to worship the Lord, refused to give up the gods of their homelands. Moreover, the few Israelites who were left behind intermarried with the people from these foreign nations. As a result, the people of Samaria were not considered true Israelites, and in the time of Jesus, the Jews refused to associate with them. This explains why the Jews were so surprised to hear Jesus' parable of the good Samaritan.

So how was Samaria founded? The Scriptures actually tell us. During his reign, King Omri, the sixth king of Israel, bought a piece of property from a man named Shemer and built a city on it, calling it Samaria. In her book, *Archaeology in the Holy Land*, Dame Kathleen Kenyon, late president of the Oxford University Archaeological Society, stated: "[The] excavation confirms the biblical account that Omri founded his town [Samaria] on a virgin site . . . The floor levels associated with his buildings rest directly upon rock."

Once again archaeology confirms the biblical narrative.

SHECHEM

GENESIS 11:27–12:11

Abram traveled through the land as far as the site of the great tree of Moreh at Shechem. At that time the Canaanites were in the land. The Lord appeared to Abram and said, "To your offspring I will give this land." So he built an altar there to the Lord, who had appeared to him.

(GENESIS 12:6-7)

ITEM FOUND: City ruins

DISCOVERED: 1903

LOCATION: Tel Balatah, thirty-five miles north of Jerusalem (M1 and M3)

EXPEDITION: Dr. Hermann Thiersch

Revered by Jews, Christians, and Muslims alike, Abraham was originally from Ur, in modern-day Iraq. After he got married, he, his wife Sarah, his father, and his nephew Lot moved to Haran, in modern-day Turkey. In those days, both Iraq and southern Turkey were part of one region, known as Mesopotamia. While Abraham was living in Haran, God asked him to leave his father's household, his people, and his country, and move to Canaan, modern-day Israel. Abraham obediently departed with his wife Sarah and his nephew Lot in tow. They went into the land of Canaan (M3) as far south as Shechem, and it was there that the Lord told Abraham that He would give that land to Abraham's offspring as their inheritance (see also "Hebron"). Abraham settled among the Hittites in Hebron, where he and many members of his family are buried today.

Shechem was also the location where Jacob had bought some land to settle in after he had left his father-in-law's house in Mesopotamia. He built an altar and worshipped God here. Unfortunately, Jacob's sons murdered all the male inhabitants because the son of the prince of that area had premarital sex with their sister, Dinah.

In 1050 BC, God's people foolishly asked for an earthly king to rule them. God gave them Saul, David, and Solomon. After King Solomon's death in 970 BC, the united nation of Israel split into two kingdoms or tribes: the southern tribe of Judah and the northern tribe of Israel. Shechem was the first capital of the northern tribe of Israel.

Around AD 30 Jesus went to Shechem and spoke to a Samaritan woman by the Well of Jacob. He explained to her that salvation is from the Jews, meaning that He Himself is the One who saves, because He is the promised Messiah, the Christ.

In his book, *Cities of the Biblical World*, LaMoine F. DeVries, who holds a PhD from Southern Baptist Theological Seminary, said:

> Shechem is perhaps best described as a community of sacred places and traditions. It was one of the major religious and political centers in ancient Israel. During the united monarchy Shechem was second only to Jerusalem as a major religious and political center. . . . The Bible, extra-biblical sources, and archaeological discoveries confirm ancient Shechem of the Canaanite, Israelite, and Samaritan periods as a city of altars, sacred pillars and trees, temples, covenants, covenant renewal, and political confirmation ceremonies.

Today, Shechem is an archaeological site located right next to the modern city of Nablus, in the northern West Bank (see M3).

SUSA

BOOK OF ESTHER

Now there was in the citadel of Susa a Jew of the tribe of Benjamin, named Mordecai son of Jair, the son of Shimei, the son of Kish, who had been carried into exile from Jerusalem by Nebuchadnezzar king of Babylon, among those taken captive with Jehoiachin king of Judah. (ESTHER 2:5-6)

ITEM FOUND: City ruins

DISCOVERED: 1851

LOCATION: Shush, Iran, about eighty miles north of Abadan, Iran (M4)

EXPEDITION: William Kenneth Loftus

In the fifth century BC a Babylonian king named Xerxes ruled the city of Susa. He was very wealthy and ruled over more than 120 provinces. Perhaps out of generosity, or maybe vanity, Xerxes decided to display his wealth during 180 days of festivities. At the end of this time he hosted a seven-day banquet for all his subjects living in the citadel. On the last day, Xerxes was quite full of himself and very drunk. In his compromised condition, he decided to show off the last treasure he had: his very beautiful wife, Vashti. Vashti was in the middle of hosting her own banquet for the women, and being the well-bred queen that she was, refused to be displayed like a prizewinning head of cattle in front of all the men of the citadel, who were probably as intoxicated as her husband. Her refusal to appear in front of the men caused a great stir. The king's advisors insisted that Vashti be removed from the throne as a warning to the other women that they had better never disobey their husbands the way Vashti did.

Through a series of events, a new bride was chosen for King Xerxes. Her name was Esther. Esther was the woman through whom the Lord saved his people from the wrath and hatred of a high official named Haman. Haman hated the Jews and had cleverly devised a way to eliminate them. But Esther put her trust in God, and Haman's plans were foiled. Furthermore, the evil plans he made for the Jews fell on him and his family, and the Jews survived another attempted annihilation.

Susa, or Shushan, one of the ancient cities of the Babylonians, where Esther and Xerxes lived, was the capital of Elam. This kingdom was located in southwestern Persia, modern-day Iran, by the riverbanks of Kerkha. Susa is mentioned numerous times in Babylonian texts of the third millennium BC, and archaeology has revealed that in the day of Esther it was probably about thirty thousand to forty thousand acres in size. Currently, the ruins cover a mere five thousand acres, but they hold a wealth of archaeological treasures, including a citadel-mound dated to the fifth century BC. In the *Archaeological Encyclopedia of the Holy Land*, Avraham Negev, who holds a PhD from Hebrew University in Jerusalem, had this to say about what was unearthed: "[Susa] was subdivided into four districts: a fortified mound . . . a royal city with the palaces of Darius and his successors; and two quarters for artisans, merchants and others, the last occupying the right bank of the river . . . The earliest settlement at the site goes back to the fourth millennium BC, from which time a ziggurat (tower-temple) erected on an extremely large brick-built platform has survived."

Today, Shush is the modern name for Susa. It is the administrative capital of the Shush County of Iran's Khuzestan Province and has a population of more than sixty-five thousand people.

TYRE

2 SAMUEL 5

Now Hiram king of Tyre sent messengers to David, along with cedar logs and carpenters and stonemasons, and they built a palace for David. And David knew that the LORD had established him as king over Israel and had exalted his kingdom for the sake of his people Israel. (2 SAMUEL 5:11–12)

ITEM FOUND: City ruins

DISCOVERED: 1948

LOCATION: Tyre, fifty miles south of Beirut, Lebanon (M3)

EXPEDITION: General Directorate of Antiquities

Tyre is an ancient Phoenician island port city in Lebanon, built on rocky terrain. It was established around 2750 BC, and its name has been found on monuments dated to as early as 1300 BC.

The Bible first introduces us to Tyre when Joshua and the Israelites leave the desert to conquer the territories of the Canaanites. In due time, each of the twelve tribes of Israel inherited portions of their conquests. Tyre was among the twenty-two towns and villages given to the tribe of Asher. Later, when David was anointed king over Israel, Hiram, king of Tyre, wished to congratulate him on his accession to the throne. So to pay tribute to him, Hiram offered David the services of his workmen and the building materials necessary to erect a beautiful palace for his use. At this time, Tyre was very wealthy due to her exclusive purple dye industry, her colonization of territories around the Mediterranean, and her maritime trade. But perhaps the most interesting fact about Tyre is that the prophet Ezekiel prophesied about its destruction more than two hundred years before it happened.

It seems that God was angry with the Tyrians because they rejoiced at the devastation of Jerusalem under Nebuchadnezzar II. It was not that Tyre was an enemy of the Jews; rather, they envisioned a further increase of prosperity and wealth for themselves because all those who used to go to Jerusalem for trade and commerce would now go to Tyre instead. The attitude of prospering on the demise of someone else is directly against God's teaching of loving and serving one another. Therefore, God spoke against Tyre. Ezekiel's prophecy included a great army that would tear down Tyre's fortified walls and towers and put the people to death by the sword. They would be plundered and looted, their homes destroyed, and all of Tyre's stones, timber, and rubble would be thrown into the sea. The final part of the prophecy was that Tyre would never be rebuilt.

In 332 BC every word of this prophecy came true when Alexander the Great besieged and destroyed Tyre. The city's rubble, which he threw into the sea to build a causeway to the mainland, is still intact to this day, and the island city has never been rebuilt.

When Jesus visited the mainland portion of Tyre, it had become a Roman province. It was here that Jesus healed a woman's daughter of demon possession (see Matthew 15:21–28).

In the book *The Jewish Past Revisited: Reflections on Modern Jewish Historians*, Israeli biblical scholar Sara Japhet, who holds a PhD from Hebrew University in Jerusalem, said:

> Not only the geographical but also the historical-geographical aspect of the biblical stories are confirmed by archeological surveys and excavations. Sites are found where they are expected to be, and information is confirmed about the various peoples and states that surrounded Israel throughout the Bronze and Iron Ages. Moab, Ammon, Edom, Tyre, the various Armean states, Arabs, Philistines and more all appear at exactly the places and times where the Bible places them.

Today, the island of Tyre (also called Soûr) is open to the public. The ruins include mosaic streets, public baths, the foundations of a Crusader cathedral, and civic buildings. There is also a Roman hippodrome, which was declared a World Heritage Site in 1979 in an effort to preserve its remains from being damaged or destroyed.

UR OF THE CHALDEANS

NEHEMIAH 9-10

"You are the Lord God, who chose Abram and brought him out of Ur of the Chaldeans and named him Abraham. You found his heart faithful to you, and you made a covenant with him to give to his descendants the land of the Canaanites, Hittites, Amorites, Perizzites, Jebusites and Girgashites. You have kept your promise because you are righteous." (NEHEMIAH 9:7-8)

ITEM FOUND: A royal cemetery

DISCOVERED: 1922

LOCATION: Southern Iraq (M4)

EXPEDITION: Leonard Woolley, 1922–1935

It is amazing how an entire civilization can disappear under sand and rubble. Many of the cities and towns mentioned in the Bible have suffered this fate, and Ur was one of them.

Located in Mesopotamia, ancient Ur was known as Ur of the Chaldeans. This was where Abraham lived before God called him to "leave your country, your people and your father's household and go to the land I will show you" (Genesis 12:1). It is located about halfway between Baghdad, Iraq, and the Persian Gulf. This was once a fertile land, and around 3000 BC it was the capital of a wealthy empire, which is witnessed by the Ziggurat, which still stands today.

Today, Ur is identified with Tell el-Muqayyar, the "Mound of Pitch." Besides uncovering parts of the city and the temple area, archaeologists have unearthed a royal cemetery filled with objects and ornaments created from gold, silver, and precious stones. In his book, *The Bible as History*, the late German journalist Werner Keller said, "Ur of the Chaldees was a powerful, prosperous, colourful and busy capital city at the beginning of the second millennium B.C."

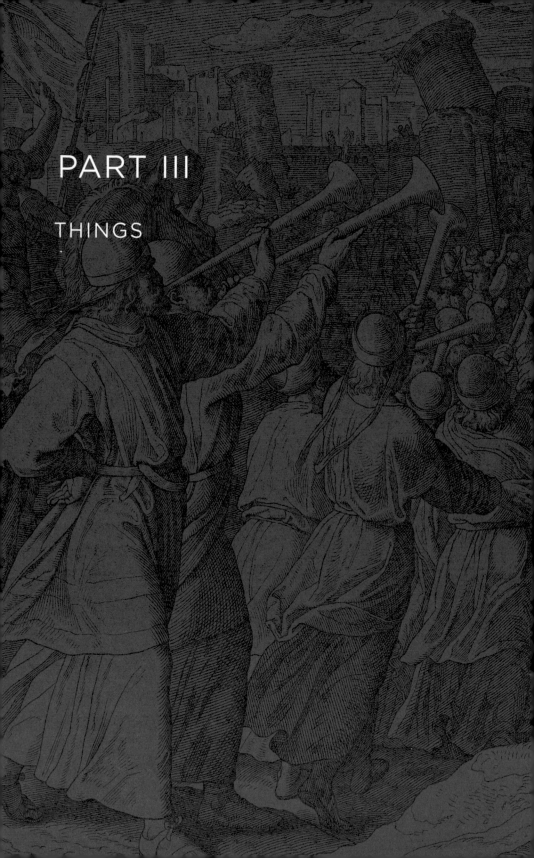

PART III

THINGS

AHAB'S HOUSE OF IVORY

1 KINGS 22

As for the other events of Ahab's reign, including all he did, the palace he built and inlaid with ivory, and the cities he fortified, are they not written in the book of the annals of the kings of Israel? (1 KINGS 22:39)

ITEM FOUND: Ivory plaque

DISCOVERED: 1931–1935

LOCATION: Samaria, Israel (M3)

EXPEDITION: Harvard University

Many people have heard the name Jezebel, which has become synonymous with a wayward woman. But they probably do not realize that Jezebel was an actual person who was married to a man named Ahab. Ahab was an Israelite king who was greatly influenced by his Phoenician wife. Under Jezebel's direction Ahab denied the God of Israel, employing hundreds of Baal and Asherah prophets and setting up idols for worship. Their story is most noted for the confrontation between Elijah, the man of God, and the prophets of Baal and Asherah, in which Elijah, by God's hand, wins a decisive victory (see 1 Kings 18).

Ahab's story mentions a palace adorned with ivory. Phoenicians were known for, among other things, their ivory industry. Here is what Dr. Michael Avi-Yonah, who earned his PhD from the University of London, had to say in his book, *A History of Israel and the Holy Land*: "Israel's general prosperity at that time is manifest in the fortifications at Samaria and in the palace of the Omride dynasty; fragments of ivory discovered in the palace confirm the tale of the house of ivory which Ahab built."

Archaeologists, digging in Samaria at Ahab's palace complex, uncovered more than five hundred fragments depicting flowers and animals, winged figures in human form, and the Egyptian gods Isis and Horus.

BOAT

MATTHEW 13:1-23

That same day Jesus went out of the house and sat by the lake. Such large crowds gathered around him that he got into a boat and sat in it, while all the people stood on the shore. Then he told them many things in parables. (MAT-THEW 13:1-3)

ITEM FOUND: A two-thousand-year-old fishing boat

DISCOVERED: 1986

LOCATION: Northwestern shore of the Sea of Galilee, Israel (M3)

EXPEDITION: Shelley Wachsmann and Kurt Raveh of the Israel Department of Antiquities

Throughout time, ships and boats have played an integral part in society. From war ships to cargo ships to travel ships, at least one of these vessels appears in every history book. This is even the case in the New Testament.

The book of Matthew introduces us to several fishermen who are tending to their fishing boats and nets by the Sea of Galilee. These fishermen become some of Jesus' disciples. Later on, we find Jesus in a boat with the disciples during a frightening storm, teaching them a lesson about faith and trust. As the narrative progresses we read that as Jesus' fame grew, the crowds that came to see Him were so big He had to teach them the truths of God from a boat while the people stood on the shore.

Now, jump ahead two thousand years. On the beaches near Kibbutz Ginosar on the northwestern side of the Sea of Galilee, two brothers, Moshe and Yuval Lufan, spent their days looking for artifacts, such as ancient coins, which occasionally washed ashore. As God would have it, there had been a two-year drought in Israel, which caused the water levels to drop. This exposed the first ancient boat ever to be found here. The brothers contacted the Israel Department of Antiquities, and an emergency excavation began.

The Galilee Boat, also known as the Jesus Boat, was built using seven different kinds of wood and measures approximately twenty-seven feet long by seven feet wide. The term *Jesus Boat* was given to the vessel not because it belonged to Jesus personally but because it has been identified as a boat from Jesus' time. Here's what archaeologist Shelley Wachsmann, who holds a PhD from Hebrew University in Jerusalem, had to say: "The boat's dating was determined by the techniques used in its construction, by pottery found in its proximity, by a battery of carbon-14 tests and by its historical considerations. . . [These] strongly suggest that the boat was in use on the Sea of Galilee between 100 BCE and 67 CE."

Today, you can visit the boat at the Yigal Allon Museum at Ginosar in Israel.

DRACHMAS

NEHEMIAH 7:1-73

SOME OF THE HEADS OF THE FAMILIES contributed to the work. The governor gave to the treasury 1,000 drachmas of gold, 50 bowls and 530 garments for priests. Some of the heads of the families gave to the treasury for the work 20,000 drachmas of gold and 2,200 minas of silver. The total given by the rest of the people was 20,000 drachmas of gold, 2,000 minas of silver and 67 garments for priests.

(NEHEMIAH 7:70-72)

ITEM FOUND: Coins

DISCOVERED: 1931

LOCATION: Beth-zur, South of Jerusalem (M3)

EXPEDITION: Dr. William F. Albright

Today when we think of money, we usually do not get much farther than the thought of what that money can buy us. But in fact, there is a lot more to currency than we realize. Currency projects a nation's sovereignty, documents its history, and controls its economy. Archaeologically, coins can tell us a lot about a people; who the rulers were during a certain time period, and how advanced they were in their world economy. It is in this light that we celebrate the discovery of the drachma at Beth-zur.

In the book of Nehemiah, we read that a contribution of one thousand drachmas was given to the Temple treasury. But for years scholars argued that Nehemiah, who lived around 450 BC, could not have written about this Greek coinage. They thought that these coins would not have reached Palestine until after 330 BC. Therefore, they decided that the book of Nehemiah was written somewhere around 250 BC by some unknown author. However, once again, through archaeology, the Bible proves accurate. In their book *Archaeology and Bible History*, the late Dr. Joseph Free, who held a PhD from Princeton University, and Dr. Howard Vos, who holds a PhD from Northwestern University, wrote, "The excavators found in the Persian level (c. 530–330 BC) six drachma coins, proving that the drachma was known in Palestine in the Persian period and that Nehemiah could have mentioned it about 450 BC without being 'ahead of himself.'" Additionally, the Elephantine papyri show that the drachma was the standard coinage in Palestine during the period between 450 and 330 BC.

HEZEKIAH'S RESERVOIR

2 CHRONICLES 32:1-23

"You built a reservoir between the two walls for the water of the Old Pool, but you did not look to the One who made it, or have regard for the One who planned it long ago." (ISAIAH 22:11)

ITEM FOUND: A reservoir outside of Hezekiah's Tunnel

DISCOVERED: End of the nineteenth century

LOCATION: Jerusalem (M2 and M3)

EXPEDITION: Blis Vediki

Hezekiah was twenty-five when he became king over Judah, and he reigned for twenty-nine years. He was a good king and very faithful to the Lord. He destroyed all the sacred stones and Asherah poles, tore down all the high places and altars, and reestablished the service of the Lord's temple. Because of this, the Lord blessed everything Hezekiah put his hands to.

In the fourteenth year of Hezekiah's reign, Sennacherib, king of Assyria, invaded Judah. To impede Sennacherib's army from conquering Jerusalem, Hezekiah decided to cut off the water supply that flowed from the springs outside the city as well as the stream that flowed throughout the land and collect it inside the city walls into a reservoir that he and his people could easily access. He also constructed a tunnel to conceal the water flow and reservoir.

In 1880, in the Old City of Jerusalem, a boy bathing in the water discovered an inscription on the tunnel walls, which was left behind by the tunnelers. It detailed the events that took place during its construction (see also "Hezekiah's Tunnel").

This reservoir has been called the Pool of Siloam, but a recent find leads many to believe that this pool is not necessarily the pool that Jesus referred to in John 9. While it may seem at the moment that there are two pools of Siloam—one from the Second Temple period (536 BC–AD 70) and one from the Byzantine era (AD 330–1453)—archaeology may soon show us that these two pools are actually connected as one. This is what David L. Chandler of the *Boston Globe* had to say about Hezekiah's reservoir: "Today, 2,700 years later, the tunnel Hezekiah built to save the city still works, and the waters of the spring of Gihon, outside the ancient city walls, still flow through Hezekiah's Tunnel to the [pool]."

The reservoir (pool) is 240 by 140 feet and can hold three million gallons of water. (For the pool mentioned by Jesus, see "Pool of Siloam.")

HEZEKIAH'S TUNNEL

2 CHRONICLES 32

As for the other events of Hezekiah's reign, all his achievements and how he made the pool and the tunnel by which he brought water into the city, are they not written in the book of the annals of the kings of Judah? (2 KINGS 20:20-21)

ITEM FOUND: Water tunnel

DISCOVERED: 1838

LOCATION: Southeast corner of present-day Jerusalem (M2 and M3)

EXPEDITION: Edward Robinson and Eli Smith

In 701 BC King Hezekiah decided to build an underground water tunnel to protect the city's water supply from their Assyrian enemies. Sennacherib was on his way to Jerusalem to make war with the Israelite king, and since water was desperately needed for survival, the people of the city got straight to work. The idea was to construct a tunnel that would not only cut off the water supply from its source, the Gihon Spring, but to redirect it into the city without being detected from the outside.

This half-mile, S-shaped, underground dig was successfully completed, and as translated by Émile Puech, who holds a PhD in history and religious anthropology from Sorbonne University, the workers memorialized and celebrated their joy by chiseling the following into the side of the tunnel: "Behold the tunnel, this is the story of its cutting. While the miners swung their picks, one toward the other . . . the voice of one calling his fellow was heard. . . . So the day they broke through, the miners struck, one against the other, pick against pick, and the water flowed from the spring towards the pool, 1,200 cubits. The height of the rock above the head of the miners was 100 cubits." This tunnel was a key to foiling Sennacherib's plans to mount a successful siege because the conquering army could not survive without water.

According to the Hebrew University of Jerusalem, "Modern radiometric dating of the Siloam [Hezekiah's] Tunnel in Jerusalem shows that it was excavated about 700 years before the Common Era, and can thus be safely attributed to the Judean King Hezekiah. This is the first time that a structure mentioned in the Bible (Kings II 20:20; Chronicles II 32:3, 4) has been radiometrically dated."

HIGH PLACE

2 KINGS 17

"The Israelites secretly did things against the Lord their God that were not right. From watchtower to fortified city they built themselves high places in all their towns. They set up sacred stones and Asherah poles on every high hill and under every spreading tree. At every high place they burned incense, as the nations whom the LORD had driven out before them had done. They did wicked things that provoked the LORD to anger. They worshiped idols, though the LORD had said, "You shall not do this." (2 KINGS 17:9-13)

ITEM FOUND: Open-air platform used for pagan worship

DISCOVERED: 1976

LOCATION: Tel Dan, Israel (M3)

EXPEDITION: Avraham Biran

In ancient Israel, "high places" were places of prayer or sacrifice, typically located on a hill or elevated platform. In the prophet Samuel's day, when there was no temple, it was perfectly acceptable to worship the Lord at a high place, but once the Temple had been built, it was no longer allowed. In disobedience, northern Israel continued to use high places to worship the Lord, but they also used them to worship and sacrifice to the false Canaanite gods, and so fell into great sin.

In 1976, one such high place was discovered in Tel Dan. According to Richard Ostling, former chief religion writer for the Associated Press, who holds an MA in religion from Northwestern University:

[Archaeologist] Biran believes this was an open-air shrine of the type often referred to in the Bible as a "bamah" or "high place." The entire complex was probably what 1 Kings 12 and other passages call a "beit-bamat," meaning "house of high places." Identification of the site was confirmed in part through the discovery of cult objects associated with shrines: oil lamps with seven wicks, a stand for burning sacred incense, a bowl containing animal bones, figurines and large containers decorated with snakes, a symbol associated with pagan worship of the nature god Baal.

The ruins feature a platform, about sixty feet wide, constructed of large blocks of stone, reminiscent of the biblical description.

HORNS OF THE ALTAR

1 KINGS 1-2

At this, all Adonijah's guests rose in alarm and dispersed. But Adonijah, in fear of Solomon, went and took hold of the horns of the altar. Then Solomon was told, "Adonijah is afraid of King Solomon and is clinging to the horns of the altar. He says, 'Let King Solomon swear to me today that he will not put his servant to death with the sword.'"

(1 KINGS 1:49-51)

ITEM FOUND: A horned altar

DISCOVERED: 1973

LOCATION: Northern Negev, Israel, several kilometers east of the present-day city of Beersheba (M2 and M3)

EXPEDITION: Yohanan Aharoni 1969–1976

As King David lay on his deathbed, one of his sons, named Adonijah, decided to try to take succession of the throne. He had a feast with all his brothers and the royal officials of Judah, but he did not invite his half brother Solomon, or any of King David's closest advisers. When David heard about this, he quickly gave orders to his men; his priest, Zadok; and the prophet Nathan to establish his son Solomon as God's anointed king. When they had done so, they sent word to Adonijah, and he was so afraid for his life that he ran to grab hold of the horns of the altar, fully expecting to be spared. Solomon did spare Adonijah and gave him a chance to show himself worthy, but in due time Adonijah revealed that he still intended to take the throne. So, Solomon had him killed for treason against God and man.

In the Bible, there are two kinds of horned altars, used for different purposes. One was a square altar of incense made of acacia wood and covered in gold. The horns of the altar were one with it, and this altar was located just outside the sanctuary. It was used to cleanse the high priest of his sin and to cleanse the people of sins they had committed unknowingly.

The other horned altar was covered in bronze and was also used to cleanse the people of their sin. But this particular type of altar was also a place where someone could go to seek protection, just as Adonijah had done. Interestingly, it was an altar such as this that was used to consecrate Aaron and his sons to the priesthood of God (Exodus 27-29).

Jump ahead three thousand years to 1973. According to the American Schools of Oriental Research, the ruins of a four-horned altar were found in Beersheba, embedded in a restored storehouse wall dated to the eighth century BC.

In his book, *Archaeology of the Bible: Book by Book*, Gaalyah Cornfeld said, "Even such a small detail as the horns of the altar [1 Kings 2:28] has now been confirmed by archaeological discoveries at Megiddo, Dan and Beersheba."

JEHOIAKIM'S PALACE

JEREMIAH 22

"Woe to him who builds his palace by unrighteousness, his upper rooms by injustice, making his countrymen work for nothing, not paying them for their labor. He says, 'I will build myself a great palace with spacious upper rooms.' So he makes large windows in it, panels it with cedar and decorates it in red." (JEREMIAH 22:13-14)

ITEM FOUND: Palace ruins

DISCOVERED: 1959–1962

LOCATION: Ramat Rahel, halfway between Jerusalem and Bethlehem (M3)

EXPEDITION: Yohanan Aharoni

Jehoiakim became king of Judah at the age of twenty-five and reigned in Jerusalem for eleven years. He was a selfish and evil king who took advantage of his subjects for his own gain and glory. For example, he built a palace for himself using forced labor, and he extorted money from his people to pay tribute to the Babylonian king Nebuchadnezzar. Worse yet, the Bible says he followed in the footsteps of Manasseh, meaning that he worshipped idols and murdered innocent people. Through the prophet Jeremiah, God had warned Jehoiakim and all Israel that they needed to repent and turn from their ways. But when Jehoiakim heard the warning message, he took the scroll upon which was written God's prophetic word and burned it. In response, God pronounced that Jehoiakim's reign would end and no one from his family would succeed him. Furthermore, everyone associated with him, as well as everyone living in Judah, would be punished for their refusal to respect, honor, or obey the Lord.

More than twenty-five hundred years later, an archaeologist named Yohanan Aharoni and his team were digging in Ramat Rahel, which lies between Bethlehem and Jerusalem. The mound revealed something amazing because it was the first time a royal palace and fortress of one of the Judean kings had been unearthed. Here is what Leah Bronner, doctor of ancient Semitic languages and history from the University of Judaism, said in her book *Biblical Personalities and Archaeology*: "All factors indicate that one of the Judean kings converted this site into a large fortress, in the center of which he built a magnificent palace. In the light of the archaeological evidence this can only be one of the last kings and a reference to the building of a palace by Jehoiakim, who ruled about 608–587 B.C.E., [and] is preserved in the Book of Jeremiah."

The palace that was discovered has many of the features mentioned in the book of Jeremiah, including large rooms with cut-out windows and red paint. Furthermore, excavators uncovered a potsherd bearing a drawing of a king, which likely represents Jehoiakim, making it the second "photo" of a biblical king in existence. (The other is of the northern king Jehu.)

JEZREEL PALACE

1 KINGS 21

[Naboth's] vineyard was in Jezreel, close to the palace of Ahab king of Samaria. Ahab said to Naboth, "Let me have your vineyard to use for a vegetable garden, since it is close to my palace." (1 KINGS 21:1-2)

ITEM FOUND: Palace ruins

DISCOVERED: 1990–1991

LOCATION: Northern Israel (M3)

EXPEDITION: David Ussishkin

Ahab was the seventh king of Israel, and he ruled twenty-two years, from about 876 to 854 BC. He married a Phoenician woman named Jezebel in order to gain an alliance with a nation well known for its successful commerce. Later, he married off his daughter, Athaliah, to the prince of Judah, thereby reestablishing good relations with the southern tribes. Unfortunately, Ahab was not as concerned with his relationship with the Lord. He built a temple and an altar to the Phoenician god Baal, which pleased his wife but provoked the Lord to anger. Furthermore, Ahab allowed Jezebel to tear down the altars of the Lord and kill His prophets.

Ahab's main residence was in Samaria, but he also had a winter palace on a small hilltop overlooking the Jezreel Valley. One day,

Ahab noticed a vineyard near his winter palace and thought that it would make the perfect location for a vegetable garden. Although on the surface it would seem that Ahab's desire to purchase the plot of land was innocent, it was not. God had commanded that whatever land had been given to a family or tribe during the division of Canaan after the exodus, was not to be sold off, even to another Israelite. Naboth, the owner of the property, knew God's law and refused to sell his vineyard to the king. When Jezebel heard about the dilemma, she devised a scheme to have Naboth murdered. When the evil deed was done, Ahab went and took the property. Because of this, the Lord proclaimed that disaster would be visited upon Ahab's descendants and that Jezebel would be devoured by dogs on Naboth's land. These prophecies were fulfilled in due time as recorded in 2 Kings 9.

In 1990, under the direction of archaeologist David Ussishkin, a royal palace was unearthed in Jezreel. In his book *What Did the Bible Writers Know and When Did They Know It?*, archaeologist William Dever wrote, "The remarkable size of the enclosures, the deep, elaborate constructional fills on which it was erected, the casemate defense walls, and the use of alternating 'pilasters' of dressed ashlar masonry are all typical features that would be found only in royal constructions." Dever further stated, "The results provide another remarkable convergence with biblical accounts."

PETER'S HOUSE

MARK 1:29-39

As soon as they left the synagogue, they went with James and John to the home of Simon and Andrew. Simon's mother-in-law was in bed with a fever, and they told Jesus about her. So he went to her, took her hand and helped her up. The fever left her and she began to wait on them.

(MARK 1:29-31)

ITEM FOUND: Ruins of a house

DISCOVERED: 1968

LOCATION: Capernaum, Israel (M3)

EXPEDITION: Fathers Virgilio Corbo and Stanislao Loffreda

Capernaum was a small fishing village near the northern shore of the Sea of Galilee. It was the hometown of the apostles Peter, Andrew, James, John, and Matthew. Scripture indicates that on one particular occasion, after teaching in the synagogue, Jesus went to Peter's house. Peter's mother-in-law was sick with fever, and He healed her, along with many others who came to Him later that evening. On another occasion, Jesus was teaching the crowd that had gathered at Peter's home and a paralytic was brought to Him. But because there were so many people in attendance, the man's friends opened a hole in the roof and lowered the man right in front of Jesus. Jesus forgave the man's sins, and the people accused Him, in their hearts, of blasphemy because He was claiming to be able to do something that only God himself can do. So, Jesus asked them if it was easier to say "Your sins are forgiven" or to heal a paralytic. To prove that He had the authority to forgive sins because He was in fact God, He told the paralytic to get up and walk home. In view of all, the man rose up and walked out. What further proof does Jesus need to show the world that He was—and is—who He claimed to be: God?

In 1968, in the city of Capernaum, two archaeologists began excavating a site located under a Byzantine church from the fourth century. This site contained an even older building under that, which had pieces of plaster with decisively Christian graffiti on them. Some pieces even had prayers and petitions written to Christ. Furthermore, among the pieces there were at least two references to Peter, also called Simon.

To determine the age of the older building, archaeologists Corbo and Loffredo began to dig under its floor. Among other things, they discovered pottery shards, fishing hooks, and oil lamps from the time of Herod Agrippa II (ca. AD 60). These items indicate that this building was once someone's home and was later converted to a house church. Another indication of this fact is that the walls were plastered, as referenced earlier, and in the first century this would have been uncommon for a home. On the other hand, it would have been a very common characteristic of a gathering place or a space for scholarly work. Additionally, many of those who had visited the house church in the fourth century said that they had "been to Peter's house which was converted to a church."

This house church continued to be used as such until the fifth century. In his book, *Is the Bible True?*, Jeffery Sheler, mentioned earlier, stated, "Many scholars now conclude that this was indeed the house of Peter, and if so the house where Jesus stayed and perhaps lived at the beginning of His ministry."

PIM

1 SAMUEL 13

Not a blacksmith could be found in the whole land of Israel, because the Philistines had said, "Otherwise the Hebrews will make swords or spears!" So all Israel went down to the Philistines to have their plowshares, mattocks, axes and sickles sharpened. The price was two thirds of a shekel [pim] for sharpening plowshares and mattocks, and a third of a shekel [shalish] for sharpening forks and axes and for repointing goads. (1 SAMUEL 13:19-21)

ITEM FOUND: A metal weight

DISCOVERED: 1902

LOCATION: Jerusalem (M2 and M3)

EXPEDITION: Professor George A. Barton

One Bible passage that remained a mystery for more than two thousand years was 1 Samuel 13:19–21. Scholars tried, in vain, to figure out what a "pim" was, but it proved impossible since no one had ever seen or heard of one before. Thankfully, to the credit of dedicated archaeologists, we now have answers.

In 1902 American Bible scholar George Barton of Bryn Mawr College discovered the first known pim to be dug out of the ground. What was it? A measure of weight! It was 7 1/2 grams, 7/8 inches long, and 5/8 inches wide. There were Hebrew inscriptions on both sides of the brassy bronze object. One side read, "Belonging to Zechariah the son of Yair," and the other side read, "pim."

A few years later, in 1907, an Irish archaeologist, R.A.S. Macalister, at Gezer in Israel, discovered another weight. It too had the word *pim* inscribed on it, but this object was made of stone. Why was one pim made of stone but the other of bronze? The answer is simple. In Samuel's day people didn't use money to purchase things. They had a kind of bartering system using weights and measures. For example, let's say you wanted to buy an ox. That ox would cost you the weight of fifteen silver shekels, which you would pay with 270 pints of barley or 265 pints of dates. If something cost one silver shekel, you would pay it with 10 pints of barley or 2 1/2 pints of oil. A pim had the weight value of two-thirds of a shekel. Therefore, when the Scriptures say the Hebrews had to pay shekels and pims for sharpening their tools, this was how it was done.

An Italian Jew named Signor Samuel Raffaeli was the first to report these findings. According to *Treasures from the Dust* by the late Azriel Eisenberg, doctor of Hebrew letters from Jewish Theological Seminary, "A year after Raffaeli made his astounding report scholars all over the world accepted it. It was a natural explanation and fit perfectly into the context of the [biblical] passage."

POMEGRANATE

EXODUS 28

"Make the robe of the ephod entirely of blue cloth, with an opening for the head in its center. There shall be a woven edge like a collar around this opening, so that it will not tear. Make pomegranates of blue, purple and scarlet yarn around the hem of the robe, with gold bells between them."

(EXODUS 28:31-33)

ITEM FOUND: An ivory pomegranate

DISCOVERED: 1979

LOCATION: Antiquities market

EXPEDITION: Unknown

In the ancient world pomegranates were among the list of delicious and coveted fruits. Kings ate them, poets wrote about them, and God used them as a sign of fertility and plenty in the land that He was giving to the Israelites. The pomegranate was eaten fresh off the tree or made into syrup for flavoring drinks. It was even made into wine. Scripture tells us that King Solomon used its image to decorate his palace and the Temple of the Lord.

When God established His priesthood through Moses' brother, Aaron, He instructed Moses to make sacred garments for him so as to bestow dignity and honor upon him. Among some of the requirements was a garment known as the robe of the ephod. Pomegranates of blue, purple, and scarlet yarn were to be placed along its hem, and bells of gold were to be hung between them so the sound could be heard whenever Aaron walked into the Holy Place to minister before the Lord. This was also to be done to ensure that Aaron would not die.

Here is what David Briggs, former writer for the Associated Press, who holds an MA in religion from Yale Divinity School, said when an ivory pomegranate surfaced in Israel:

> [The pomegranate] was discovered in 1979 at the shop of an antiquities dealer and was later sold to the Israel Museum in 1988 by sellers who remained anonymous. What ties the scepter to Solomon's Temple is an inscription that has been translated as "Holy to the priests, belonging to the House of Yahweh," according to the catalog from the Smithsonian exhibition. . . . The finds provide contrary evidence to . . . a "nihilist" school of biblical scholarship that would claim all events described in the Bible before the Babylonian exile are fictional.

POOL OF BETHESDA

JOHN 5:1-15

Now there is in Jerusalem near the Sheep Gate a pool, which in Aramaic is called Bethesda and which is surrounded by five covered colonnades. Here a great number of disabled people used to lie—the blind, the lame, the paralyzed. One who was there had been an invalid for thirty-eight years. When Jesus saw him lying there and learned that he had been in this condition for a long time, he asked him, "Do you want to get well?" (JOHN 5:1-6)

ITEM FOUND: A pool

DISCOVERED: 1888

LOCATION: Near the Sheep's Gate, Jerusalem (M3)

EXPEDITION: Herr Conrad Schick

In the fifth chapter of the book of John, the author recounts one of Jesus' many miracles. While in Jerusalem for one of the Jewish feasts, Jesus decided to go to the Pool of Bethesda, which was near the Sheep's Gate. The word *Bethesda* means "house of mercy," and this pool was known for its curative properties. Many of the lame, the blind, and the crippled would lie by the water in hopes of being cured. Jesus approached one of the invalids there and asked him if he wanted to get well. The man replied that in thirty-eight years, he'd had no one to help him into the water whenever it was divinely stirred. Then Jesus, the Great Physician, and Friend to sinners, spoke the words, "Get up! Pick up your mat and walk." Instantly the man was made whole. This miracle is only mentioned in the book of John.

For centuries the Pool of Bethesda was lost to history and therefore thought by some to be fictional. But in 1888 a German architect and archaeologist, Conrad Schick, discovered the pool. "Often archaeology has revealed the grounding of gospel stories that many of us thought were questionable," said James Charlesworth, doctor of New Testament and Syriac from Duke University. "For example, John's gospel mentions the Pool at Bethsaida [Bethesda], which has five porticoes [colonnades]. Now all the experts swore this couldn't exist because a pentagon was not found in ancient architecture "Perhaps the five porticoes were just a symbol for the five books of the Pentateuch. Then archaeologists began to dig-one of the Dead Sea Scrolls describes exactly where Bethsaida would have been. And sure enough, there are five places for porticoes: north, south, east, west and one portico in the center between the two huge pools."

Located in the Old City, north of the Temple Mount, the Pool of Bethesda is open to the public.

POOL OF GIBEON

2 SAMUEL 2-4

Abner son of Ner, together with the men of Ish-Bosheth son of Saul, left Mahanaim and went to Gibeon. Joab son of Zeruiah and David's men went out and met them at the pool of Gibeon. One group sat down on one side of the pool and one group on the other side. (2 SAMUEL 2:12-13)

ITEM FOUND: A water reservoir or pool

DISCOVERED: 1956

LOCATION: Al-Jib, five miles northwest of Jerusalem
(M2 and M3)

EXPEDITION: Dr. James B. Pritchard

Five miles northwest of Jerusalem lie the ruins of the ancient city
of Gibeon. The Canaanite city of Gibeon was, at one time, as great
as one of its royal cities, and it belonged to the Hivites. Their men
were notably mighty, but when Israel entered the land after their
time of slavery in Egypt, the Gibeonites realized they were doomed.
However, because of their wit, cunning, and fear of the Lord, they
were allowed to live among the Israelites in servitude as woodcutters
and drawers of water. Furthermore, their city was allotted to the
priestly tribe of the Levites.

It was here in Gibeon that the Levites set up the tabernacle, which God had commissioned Moses to make while they were wandering in the desert. With it they set up the only God-endorsed, temporary high place for sacrifices to the Lord.

In King David's day, Gibeon continued to play an important role in the lives of the Israelites. After King Saul died in battle, the commander of his army, Abner, determined that Saul's son Ish-Bosheth (variously spelled Ishbosheth) should succeed him. But God had chosen David, and he was made king over Judah. One day, both armies met at the Pool of Gibeon. Abner suggested that each side put forward twelve men to fight to the death. Perhaps he had hoped to win the entire kingdom upon the success of his men. But both sides were so evenly matched that all twenty-four died together. It was this event, at this location, that started a battle for the united kingdom, lasting many years until Abner unwittingly gave way to God's will, leaving David king over all Israel.

In 1956, American archaeologist Dr. James B. Pritchard discovered Gibeon and its pool. After two years of excavating the pool, which was completely filled with debris, Dr. Pritchard discovered a jar handle bearing the name Gibeon. In the end, there were more than fifty jar handles found with the name Gibeon written in seventh to eighth-century Hebrew script. According to Bryant Wood, doctor of Syro-Palestinian archaeology from the University of Toronto, "[This] large pool at Gibeon is no doubt the pool where the forces of Israel's second king, David, fought under Joab against the forces of Saul's son Ishbosheth under Abner."

Today, ancient Gibeon and its pool rest side by side with the modern city of al-Jib.

POOL OF SILOAM

JOHN 9

"While I am in the world, I am the light of the world." Having said this, he [Jesus] spit on the ground, made some mud with the saliva, and put it on the [blind] man's eyes. "Go," he told him, "wash in the Pool of Siloam" (this word means Sent). So the man went and washed, and came home seeing." (JOHN 9:5-7)

ITEM FOUND: Steps to a pool

DISCOVERED: 2004

LOCATION: Silwan, southern side of Jerusalem (M2 and M3)

EXPEDITION: Eli Shukron and Ronny Reich, working with the Israel Antiquities Authority

The Pool of Siloam may be best known as the place where Jesus healed a blind man by putting mud on his eyes and then having him wash it off in the pool. However, this pool is also mentioned in Nehemiah as an area near the city wall that the Jews had worked at restoring after they had returned from captivity circa 515 BC.

In 2004, while the city of Jerusalem was carrying out infrastructure work for a new sewage pipe, they uncovered steps to a water reservoir. This reservoir is fifty yards long and lined with stones. The steps lead into it from all sides. Archaeologists and the Antiquities Authority say that this is the Pool of Siloam mentioned by Jesus, and date it to the Second Temple period (536 BC–AD 70).

Two thousand years ago this reservoir was used as the main source of fresh water for the city. It is fed by the Gihon Spring, just as Hezekiah's reservoir is. It is entirely possible that as the excavation continues, archaeologists may discover that Hezekiah's reservoir and the Pool of Siloam are connected as one. Archaeologist Eli Shukron, who holds an MA from the Institute of Archaeology of the Hebrew University in Jerusalem, said, "The moment that we revealed and discovered this . . . we were 100 percent sure it was the Siloam Pool." Also discovered at the site was a portion of a stone road leading from the pool to the Jewish Temple and coins from the biblical era, which helped to confirm the identity of the find. This discovery, as do all the others, continues to show that the Bible is trustworthy (also see "Hezekiah's Reservoir").

RACHEL'S TOMB

GENESIS 25:21–35:20

So Rachel died and was buried on the way to Ephrath (that is, Bethlehem). Over her tomb Jacob set up a pillar, and to this day that pillar marks Rachel's tomb." (GENESIS 35:19-20)

ITEM: Rachel's tomb

DISCOVERED: Was never lost

LOCATION: Bethlehem (M2 and M3)

EXPEDITION: None necessary

The nation of Israel began with the patriarchs Abraham, Isaac, and Jacob. Jacob had a twin brother named Esau. Because Jacob took Esau's birthright, Esau vowed to kill him and Jacob had to flee.

He escaped to the land of his mother, Rebekah. Rebekah's family lived in the city of Haran, which was in Paddan Aram in Upper Mesopotamia near modern-day Turkey. Jacob lived with his uncle Laban, who had two daughters, named Leah and Rachel. Through a series of events, Jacob ended up marrying both.

As expected, there was some sibling rivalry between the two sisters over the attention and affections of their common husband. Because Jacob loved Rachel but not Leah, the Lord had mercy on Leah, and she gave Jacob many sons while her sister, Rachel, remained barren. In anguish, Rachel cried out to the Lord, and she was finally able to conceive. She bore a son and named him Joseph.

After living in Haran for twenty years, Jacob decided it was time to go back to his own country and family. So, taking all the possessions he had acquired, he left for the land of Canaan. On the way, Rachel gave birth to her second son, named Benjamin. Because her labor had been very difficult, she died, and was buried on the way.

Rachel's tomb, unlike other biblical references, has never been lost to history. The building, which sits over the tomb, has two chambers. One is domed and has a very distinct Ottoman Muslim design. The other is an antechamber built by Sir Moses Montefiore in 1841. According to the Palestine Ministry of Tourism and Antiquities, "This small building marks the traditional Tomb of Rachel, Jacob's wife. It is considered holy to Christians, Muslims, and Jews." From 1996 to 1998 Israel fortified the site at a cost of $2 million. In 2002, a concrete wall and watchtowers were built surrounding the tomb, to protect it from aggressive vandals.

TEMPLE OF ARTEMIS

ACTS 19:23-41

"And you see and hear how this fellow Paul has convinced and led astray large numbers of people here in Ephesus and in practically the whole province of Asia. He says that man-made gods are no gods at all. There is danger not only that our trade will lose its good name, but also that the temple of the great goddess Artemis will be discredited, and the goddess herself, who is worshiped throughout the province of Asia and the world, will be robbed of her divine majesty." (ACTS 19:26-27)

ITEM FOUND: Temple ruins

DISCOVERED: 1869

LOCATION: Ephesus, Turkey (M4)

EXPEDITION: John T. Wood

One of the Seven Wonders of the World is the famed Temple of Artemis in Turkey. This structure was made of marble and housed many bronze statues, silver statuettes, and numerous works of art. People from all over the ancient world came to pay tribute to this goddess of hunting, wild nature, and fertility by leaving gifts of gold and ivory.

In the time of the apostle Paul (c. AD 5– c. 67), temple worship was the main focus of Ephesian life. However, Paul's teachings of the good news reached the hearts of his listeners to the point that they freely turned away from idol worship, burning their magical books worth fifty thousand pieces of silver each.

Over the centuries the Temple of Artemis was destroyed and rebuilt a number of times, but by AD 400 most Ephesians had turned to Christianity and the temple met its final destruction, led by John Chrysostom. Little by little the port of Ephesus silted up, and eventually the entire city was completely abandoned.

In 1863, an architect named John Wood decided he wanted to locate and excavate this wonder. It took six years and a lot of perseverance before he finally found the first evidence of the temple, fifteen feet below the ground. According to archaeologist Chris Scarre, who holds a PhD from Cambridge University, "Wood spent a further four years excavating the remains of the temple [of Artemis] and shipping back many of the sculptures to the British Museum, where they can still be seen."

TEMPLE OF THE ASHTORETHS

1 SAMUEL 31

The next day, when the Philistines came to strip the dead, they found Saul and his three sons fallen on Mount Gilboa. They cut off his head and stripped off his armor, and they sent messengers throughout the land of the Philistines to proclaim the news in the temple of their idols and among their people. They put his armor in the temple of the Ashtoreths and fastened his body to the wall of Beth Shan.

(1 SAMUEL 31:8-10)

ITEM FOUND: Temple ruins

DISCOVERED: 1923

LOCATION: Beth-Shean, Israel (M3)

EXPEDITION: University of Pennsylvania, Museum of
Archaeology and Anthropology

In Canaan during Bible times there were many gods and goddesses, with Baal and Ashtoreth as the main deities. Baal was the
sun god of storms, fertility, wine, and sex. He was worshipped on
hillsides and other high places using animal and human sacrifices. In
his temple adherents engaged in orgies, homosexuality, and sexual
acts with temple prostitutes as a form of worship. Baal's female
counterpart was the moon goddess, Ashtoreth, who originated
in Babylonia and was carried west to the Semitic tribes. She was
the goddess of erotic love and fertility, and just like Baal, she was
worshipped with ritual prostitution. These deities took on different

names in various civilizations, such as Aphrodite (Greece), Astarte (Phoenicia), and Venus (ancient Rome).

In the Scriptures, the Lord forbids His people from worshipping these deities. This is why the Bible often uses the pluralized forms of Baal and Ashtoreth (*Baalim* and *Ashtaroth*) so as to encompass all possible forms of this particular idol worship. But the people did not obey. Even King Solomon, who reigned from 970 to 930 BC, allowed himself and his wives to worship the Baals and build high places to them.

Although the Lord gave His people many warnings over a number of centuries, they continued to worship these false gods. So, He sent Israel into Assyrian captivity in 721 BC, and He sent Judah into Babylonian captivity in 586 BC. In the *Museum Journal*, Alan Rowe, late lecturer in Near Eastern archaeology at the University of Manchester in England, said, "This very house of Ashtoroth has been found. . . . The temple was erected by the Egyptians to the goddess Ashtaroth, and it was, so far as we know, the only temple intact at Beth-Shan at the time the Philistines conquered and lived in the city."

The temple is about seventy-eight feet long and sixty-two feet wide. A number of valuable artifacts were found in the temple, such as rings, earrings, ingots, and gold. There were also cult objects in the form of such things as goddesses, serpents, and birds.

THEATER OF EPHESUS

ACTS 19:23-20:1

When they heard this, they were furious and began shouting: "Great is Artemis of the Ephesians!" Soon the whole city was in an uproar. The people seized Gaius and Aristarchus, Paul's traveling companions from Macedonia, and rushed as one man into the theater. Paul wanted to appear before the crowd, but the disciples would not let him. Even some of the officials of the province, friends of Paul, sent him a message begging him not to venture into the theater. (ACTS 19:28-31)

ITEM FOUND: Theater ruins

DISCOVERED: 1863–1874

LOCATION: Ephesus, Turkey (M4)

EXPEDITION: John T. Wood

The apostle Paul had an incredible life journey. He started as a zealous Jewish Pharisee killing Christians in the name of God. Then one day, the Lord met him on the road to Damascus. It was this encounter that changed Paul's destiny forever. Paul became one of the greatest apostles of all time. He wrote virtually half of the New Testament and single-handedly reached all of Asia with the good news of the risen Messiah, "All the Jews and Greeks who lived in the province of Asia heard the word of the Lord" (Acts 19:10). But Paul's journey was not easy. It was filled with shipwrecks, beatings, prison, and an untimely death.

One noted misfortune took place in Turkey at Ephesus. Ephesus was the center for the worship of the goddess Artemis, also known as Diana. Many a shopkeeper made a living selling idols and other paraphernalia to those who worshipped her. Realizing that Paul's teachings were turning the people away from this idol worship, which ultimately cut into their sales and profits, they started a riot in the theater. According to Scripture, this disturbance lasted more than two hours until the city clerk quieted everyone down and reminded them that if they had a grievance against Paul or anyone else, they were welcome to take it to the proper authorities and deal with it in the courts. After this, everyone dispersed, and Paul left for Macedonia.

The Ephesus Theater still stands to this day. Here is how John Elder, author of *Prophets, Idols and Diggers*, described it, "The theater is situated on a hill overlooking the city, the hollow of the hill forming a natural amphitheater capable of accommodating twenty-five thousand. It had an imposing façade adorned with fine statuary. . . . A long straight road runs from the theater to the harbor. In the city there was a magnificent agora with the usual surroundings of splendid buildings, temples, colonnades and a library."

Today, the theater, the temple, and other ruins of Ephesus are open to the public.

WALLS OF JERICHO

JOSHUA 1-6

By faith the walls of Jericho fell, after the people had marched around them for seven days. (HEBREWS 11:30)

ITEM FOUND: Wall ruins

DISCOVERED: 1907

LOCATION: Jericho, Israel (M2 and M3)

EXPEDITION: German archaeologists Ernst Sellin and
Carl Watzinger

The Israelites spent forty years in the desert after they left Egypt
under Moses' leadership. This was due to their refusal to obey God
when He directed them to enter Canaan (M1) and possess the land.
Although God had promised them He would give them the victory,
the Israelites were too afraid of losing the battle that was ahead. So,
God told them that none of the men who were of military age when
they left Egypt would live to enter the promised land except for
Joshua and Caleb, who had been faithful and obedient to the Lord.

After Moses and that generation had died out, the Lord directed

Joshua, Israel's new commander, to enter the land of Canaan, as they should have done forty years earlier. So, Joshua sent two men to spy out the city of Jericho, which stood directly in their path. When the king heard that the spies were in the city, he sent men to capture them. However, a harlot named Rahab (who is later found in the ancestral line of King David and Jesus) hid the spies from the pursuers the king had sent. In return, she asked that they spare her and her family when they came back to take the city. The two spies agreed and told her that in order to be saved, anyone belonging to her needed to be in her house, which had been built into the city wall, at the time of the attack. They also instructed her to tie a scarlet cord in her window so they would know which house to spare. Rahab agreed to these terms.

As Joshua led the Israelites to the Jordan River, the Lord miraculously stopped the flow of the water, and the people crossed on dry ground. When the inhabitants of Jericho heard about what the Lord had done, their hearts "melted in fear," yet they still refused to allow the Israelites to pass peacefully. At God's direction, the people marched around the city daily for seven days, and at the sound of the priests' trumpet blast, the people gave a great shout and the walls came tumbling down. The only portion that remained standing was the one containing Rahab's house and family. The Israelites put all the inhabitants to the sword and torched the city.

Up until the twentieth century, Bible critics had doubted and mocked the idea of a city named Jericho having ever existed. They claimed that since archaeology had never found any evidence of such a site, it must have been a biblical fabrication. However, in 1907, a German archaeology team discovered the ruins of a city on a hill. They claimed it was Jericho. Since then a number of excavations have taken place there. One such excavation was headed by John Garstang from 1930 to 1936, and another was headed by the minimalist Kathleen Kenyon in the 1950s. Both British archaeologists came to the same conclusion: this was the place where the biblical Jericho once stood.

In his contribution to Sir John Alexander Hammerton's impressive tome on ancient times, archaeologist John Garstang, doctor of science from Oxford University, wrote, "In a word, in all material details and in date the fall of Jericho took place as described in the Biblical narrative . . . The walls fell, shaken apparently by earthquake, and the city was destroyed by fire, about 1400 BC. These are the basic facts resulting from our investigations." Garstang went on to describe how the bricks of the wall show evidence of "intense fire cracked stone, charred timbers, and ashes." They also found a portion of the wall, with its houses still intact. Archaeologists have determined that this section of the city was the poorer part of town because the walls were much thinner than in other parts. This lends itself to the idea that Rahab could have lived there. Excavations have also confirmed that Jericho was, in fact, the gateway to Canaan, just as the Bible purports, and that the Israelites would have had no other means of entry but through Jericho.

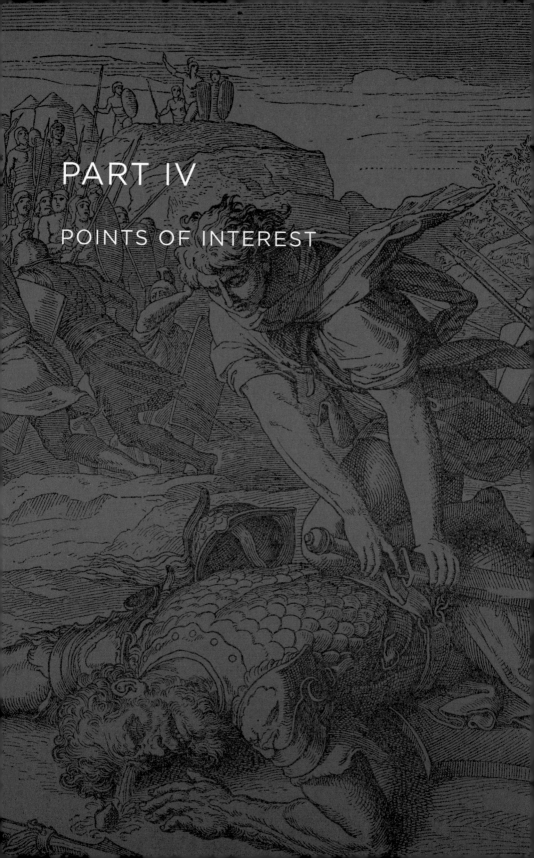

PART IV

POINTS OF INTEREST

BAAL WORSHIP

1 KINGS 16:29-33

He set up an altar for Baal in the temple of Baal that he built in Samaria. Ahab also made an Asherah pole and did more to provoke the Lord, the God of Israel, to anger than did all the kings of Israel before him. (1 KINGS 16:32-33)

ITEM FOUND: Texts

DISCOVERED: 1929

LOCATION: Ras Shamra, northern Syria (M4)

EXPEDITION: Claude F.A. Schaeffer and George Chenet

The God of Israel is a very jealous God, and He has made it clear that He will not share His glory with anyone, whether man or idol. Throughout the pages of the Bible we see this truth—for example, in the stories of (1) Herod, who allowed himself to be praised as God, so "an angel of the Lord struck him down, and he was eaten by worms and died" (Acts 12:23); and (2) the ark of God, which the marauding Philistines took to Ashdod and placed it in their temple next to their god Dagon. The next day the people found Dagon "fallen on his face on the ground before the ark of the LORD! His head and hands had been broken off and were lying on the threshold; only his body remained" (1 Samuel 5:4–5). Yet even though God has made it clear that He alone is to be worshipped, the people of Israel continued to forsake Him.

Sadly, though Israel continued to worship their God, they also worshipped Baal, the most prominent idol worshipped before the time of the exile. Baal was a Canaanite god thought to be responsible for the rain and the fertility of the earth as well as the fertility of the people. Baalism involved magic, temple prostitution, and child sacrifice. "Until early in the 20th century little was known about the Canaanite deities apart from references in the Bible. Then, in 1929, texts were discovered at Ugarit (in north Syria, now known as Ras Shamra, [M4]) . . . The gods mentioned in the texts were the same as the Canaanite ones [Baal and Ashtoreth], and their characters and stories were thus revealed for the first time," wrote Roberta L. Harris, author of *The World of the Bible*. Here is the translation of part of an unearthed text:

> So Ba'al does sit down and dwell in his palace,
> Neither king nor commoner
> on earth shall install himself on his throne!
> For I alone am king over the gods,
> give fattness to gods and men,
> satisfy the multitudes of the earth.
> Then surely calls Ba'al
> to his two pages:
> "Attend to me, Gapen and Ugar"

BRICK WITHOUT STRAW

EXODUS 5-6:1

Then the slave drivers and the foremen went out and said to the people, "This is what Pharaoh says: 'I will not give you any more straw. Go and get your own straw wherever you can find it, but your work will not be reduced at all.'" So the people scattered all over Egypt to gather stubble to use for straw. The slave drivers kept pressing them, saying, "Complete the work required of you for each day, just as when you had straw." (EXODUS 5:10-13)

ITEM FOUND: Brick walls

DISCOVERED: 1883

LOCATION: Biblical Pithom in eastern Egypt (M4)

EXPEDITION: Swiss Egyptologist Edouard Naville, with the
Egypt Exploration Fund

In the fifth chapter of the book of Exodus, we read about Moses'
commission by God to go to the Pharaoh of Egypt and demand that
he let the Israelites go. The Israelites had been in Egypt for more
than four hundred years and were treated as slaves for most of that
time. Their labor was hard, and their slave masters were cruel. The
people cried out to the Lord, and in His mercy He sent them a man
who would lead them out of Egypt and into a land flowing with
milk and honey. Moses was that man.

Unfortunately, Pharaoh did not take kindly to being told what
to do, especially by a God he did not know. Accordingly, Pharaoh

determined that the Israelites were simply complaining because they were lazy. To teach them a lesson, he decided to make them even more miserable. Pharaoh commanded that the Israelites be given no more straw to make their bricks. They were to gather it themselves while maintaining the same quota as before. Of course this work would have been impossible, and as they made their bricks without straw, the number of finished bricks dwindled.

In his book, *Voices from Rocks and Dust Heaps of Bible Lands*, J. A. Huffman, doctor of divinity from Taylor University, wrote, "Archaeology corroborates the experiences of the Israelites in Egypt described in the fifth chapter of Exodus . . . Naville, the explorer, tells us that when he excavated Pithom, one of the ancient treasure cities, he found brick in its walls made with the use of a liberal quantity of straw, some with less straw, and some without any straw."

BURNING OF HAZOR

JOSHUA 10-11

At that time Joshua turned back and captured Hazor and put its king to the sword. (Hazor had been the head of all these kingdoms.) Everyone in it they put to the sword. They totally destroyed them, not sparing anything that breathed, and he burned up Hazor itself. (JOSHUA 11:10-11)

ITEM FOUND: Structures damaged by fire

DISCOVERED: 1991

LOCATION: Tel Hazor, Israel (M2 and M3)

EXPEDITION: Amnon Ben-Tor

When the Israelites left the desert and began their takeover of Canaan, God had instructed Moses to command Joshua to totally destroy all who breathe and to leave no survivors. This was partly because the inhabitants of Canaan worshipped false gods, and the Lord did not want His people to be ensnared by their paganism. Joshua was completely faithful to his commission. In every region and in every town, he put the people and their kings to death. When the king of Hazor heard about this, he rallied all the other kings to come make war against Joshua and his army, but the Lord was with Joshua. Not only did Joshua put all the people to the sword; he also hamstrung the horses and burned the chariots as God had commanded him. Then he captured Hazor and burned it to the ground.

So, did these events happen or not? David Briggs, columnist for the Association of Religious Data Archives and a graduate of Yale Divinity School, said:

> Amnon Ben-Tor is an archeologist who doubts anything he can't dig up. He takes nothing in the Bible on faith. Yet, standing in a trench on a hot, barren mountainside, he stares into the fire-blackened stone and sees an army destroying the Canaanite city of Hazor 3,200 years ago. Just as it says in the Book of Joshua, "Hazor was destroyed by fire" when the invading Israelites claimed their Promised Land, Ben-Tor said. "Nobody can prove to me the story in Joshua is entirely fictional."

Hazor is located north of the Sea of Galilee and is the largest tell in Israel. It is also a UNESCO World Heritage site because of its cultural and historical significance.

CAMEL

GENESIS 24

Now Isaac had come from Beer Lahai Roi, for he was living in the Negev. He went out to the field one evening to meditate, and as he looked up, he saw camels approaching. Rebekah also looked up and saw Isaac. She got down from her camel and asked the servant, "Who is that man in the field coming to meet us?"

"He is my master," the servant answered. So she took her veil and covered herself. (GENESIS 24:62–65)

ITEM FOUND: Bones and text lists

DISCOVERED: various dates

LOCATION: various places

EXPEDITION: various

What is so significant about a camel when it comes to the Bible? Well, spiritually speaking, nothing. However, for Bible critics, questioning the existence of domesticated camels in Abraham's day (ca. 2000 BC) was yet another attempt to discredit the Scriptures. Critics have often said that the Old Testament was written years or centuries after the fact. In this way, they hoped to explain away the prophetic verses, their fulfillment, and even the accuracy of the smallest details concerning daily life, including biblical characters' use of the camel. Bible critics insisted that in Abraham's day there was no such thing as a domesticated camel. They decided, therefore, that Moses could not have written the book of Genesis because he would not have made that mistake. Instead, where Scriptures state that Rebekah dismounted from her camel, the book's "true author," some unknown figure from around 400 BC who did not know any better, got it wrong. They claimed that the camel was not domesticated until about the twelfth century BC.

However, on the island of Umm al Nar near Abu Dhabi, the remains of two Bactrian camels were found at an excavation site dating back to circa 2000 BC. Moreover, Mesopotamian lexical lists from the Old Babylonian period show that the camel was, in fact, domesticated by that time. Furthermore, camels' bones were also discovered in the ruins of a house at Mari of the pre-Sargonic age. These bones indicate that camels were domesticated as far back as the twenty-fifth century BC. According to Rabbi Dovid Lichtman, who holds a degree from Queens College of New York in comparative religion and philosophy and is the senior lecturer at Yeshivat Aish HaTorah, "Recent archaeological finds have clearly demonstrated that the camel was domesticated by the 18th century BCE. What was previously thought to be a knockout punch against the Bible is now evidence supporting it."

CHILD SACRIFICE

JEREMIAH 32

"They built high places for Baal in the Valley of Ben Hinnom to sacrifice their sons and daughters to Molech, though I never commanded, nor did it enter my mind, that they should do such a detestable thing and so make Judah sin." (JEREMIAH 32:35)

ITEM FOUND: Burial urns

DISCOVERED: 1921–25, 1970s

LOCATION: Carthage, North Africa (M4)

EXPEDITION: Dr. Lawrence E. Stager (1970s)

When God led His people to the promised land—that is, Canaan—He commanded them to completely destroy everything that breathes in the cities of the nations that He was giving them. He did not want His people to sin by following the detestable practices of the Canaanites, such as child sacrifice. But the Israelites did not obey God, and they allowed many of the cities' inhabitants to live. So, as added precaution, God specifically commanded the people, under penalty of death, not to sacrifice their children to the pagan Ammonite god Molech. But in time, this is exactly what the Israelites began to do. They forsook their God and burned their babies in the unholy fire of the Canaanite gods. This is one of the reasons God allowed Israel and Judah to be taken into Assyrian and Babylonian captivity.

In his book *Illustrations of Old Testament History*, the late Dr. Richard D. Barnett, longtime keeper of the British Department Museum's Department of Western Asiatic Antiquities, said:

> Discoveries in cemeteries in Carthage in 1921–25 and recently in her colonies (Sulcis, Tharros, Nora), show conclusively that it was the custom of the Carthaginian people, themselves colonists of the Phoenicians in the 8th–6th centuries B.C., to sacrifice babies by burning them on a pyre, and burying the ashes in an urn . . . There is little reason to doubt this type of human sacrifice, probably of first-born, which was practiced widely in Phoenicia and Canaan to placate the chief gods and ensure fertility of the land. Several such forms of sacrifices of male offspring were widespread among Western Semites, especially in the time of calamity. . . . The Carthaginians' custom of sacrificing their first-born children is [also] well attested from Roman authors.

Today, the burial urns of Carthage can be seen at the British Museum.

DAVID SLAYS GOLIATH

1 SAMUEL 17

As the Philistine [Goliath] moved closer to attack him, David ran quickly toward the battle line to meet him. Reaching into his bag and taking out a stone, he slung it and struck the Philistine on the forehead. The stone sank into his forehead, and he fell facedown on the ground. So David triumphed over the Philistine with a sling and a stone; without a sword in his hand he struck down the Philistine and killed him. (1 SAMUEL 17:48-50)

ITEM FOUND: Sling stones

DISCOVERED: 1996

LOCATION: Khirbet el-Maqatir, ten miles north of Jerusalem, in the West Bank (M2 and M3)

EXPEDITON: Dr. Bryant Wood (1995–Present)

Who has not heard of David and Goliath, the story of a fourteen-year-old shepherd boy who took on an eleven-foot Philistine giant, killing him with a sling and a stone? Many people have doubted this story because it doesn't seem possible that a small boy would have the strength, ability, or knowledge to compete against such a large, professional military man such as Goliath. But when reading this biblical account, there are a few things to remember. First, David was a shepherd: he was in charge of protecting his sheep against predators. David often had to fight lions and bears, which honed his battle skills. Second, David was an expert with his sling. It may not seem like an intimidating weapon, but it is deadly nonetheless.

Archaeology has shown that slings and sling stones were widely used as a military weapon during the period between about 1000 and 500 BC. Good slingers could hurl their stones more than four hundred yards, and the release speed was in excess of sixty miles an hour. Furthermore, we must erase the inaccurate perception we have of the "five smooth stones" we read about in the Bible. These stones were not mere pebbles. They were actually as large as tennis balls. Therefore, when the Scriptures say that David slung the stone at the Philistine and it sank into his forehead and killed him, we have no choice but to reach the same conclusion that *Buried History: A Quarterly Journal of Biblical Archaeology* did: "Modern archaeological research show[s] the Bible narrative to be feasible."

DEATH BY CRUCIFIXION

JOHN 18-20

So the soldiers took charge of Jesus. Carrying his own cross, he went out to the place of the Skull (which in Aramaic is called Golgotha). Here they crucified him, and with him two others—one on each side and Jesus in the middle. (John 19:16–18)

ITEM FOUND: Heel bone with nail through it

DISCOVERED: 1968

LOCATION: Northern Jerusalem (M2 and M3)

EXPEDITION: Vassilios Tzaferis, the Israel Department of Antiquities and Museums

Jesus is God not because Christians say so but because He says so. Jesus claimed His deity throughout the Scriptures in word and deed. In fact, the Jews tried to stone Jesus to death because He kept saying He was *one with the Father*: "You, a mere man, claim to be God" (John 10:33; 19:7). Jesus answered that if they could not believe His words, then they should believe all the miracles He performed, such as healing the blind, the lame, and the diseased; calming the storm; casting out demons, and much, much more.

But the human heart is wicked and dark, and it often refuses to accept the subservient position. In fact, the Jewish leaders, highly revered in that day, saw Jesus as a threat to their status and authority over the people. So, they got together and decided to arrest Him without cause and bring false charges against Him, perpetrated by false witnesses. At the end of their monkey trial, they found the Author of life guilty of blasphemy. Because they were unable to legally put him to death, they sought the aid of the Roman governor, Pontius Pilate. Although Pilate found no guilt in Jesus, and desired to free Him, he was afraid of the mob, and chose to give them what they wanted—Jesus' death on the cross.

The method of death by crucifixion was known as early as the sixth century BC and was practiced by the Persians, Seleucids, Carthaginians, and Romans. This form of execution was extremely slow and painful. The victim was typically tied or nailed to a wooden cross and left to die. First, the victim was scourged for his crime, leaving him weak from blood loss and pain. Then the victim was forced to carry his own crossbeam on his shoulders to the place where he would be crucified. This crossbeam weighed about one hundred pounds and would have been very difficult to carry, especially in a weakened condition. Once hung on the cross, the victim was left at the mercy of those who wished to verbally abuse him. Thirst, hunger, and exhaustion were constant companions, but none of this compared to the physical effects of crucifixion.

According to a study done by Mayo Clinic, because the arms of the crucified are outstretched, breathing becomes very difficult.

In time, the lungs begin to fill with fluid. The shallow breathing causes muscles to cramp, and the only way for victims to exhale is by pushing themselves up a little with their feet. This lifting of the body was excruciating because injuries on the back from the scourging would be torn open again as the victims rubbed against the wooden beam. To expedite death, victims' legs were often broken so they could no longer lift themselves, ultimately causing them to suffocate very quickly. Here is what the late Vassilios Tzaferis, doctor of classical archaeology from Hebrew University in Jerusalem, had to say in *Biblical Archaeology Review*:

> From ancient literary sources we know that tens of thousands of people were crucified in the Roman Empire . . . Yet until 1968 not a single victim of this horrifying method of execution had been uncovered archaeologically. In that year I excavated the only victim of crucifixion ever discovered . . . This practice, described in the Gospels in reference to the two thieves who were crucified with Jesus (John 19:18), has now been archaeologically confirmed.

Tzaferis described his find as a heel bone from a Jewish man who lived in Jerusalem in the first century. When this man was crucified, the nail hit a hard knot in the olive wood, causing it to bend and curl. Later, it became necessary to amputate the foot in order to remove the dead body from the cross.

GOLDEN CALF

EXODUS 32

Aaron answered them, "Take off the gold earrings that your wives, your sons and your daughters are wearing, and bring them to me." So all the people took off their earrings and brought them to Aaron. He took what they handed him and made it into an idol cast in the shape of a calf, fashioning it with a tool. Then they said, "These are your gods, O Israel, who brought you up out of Egypt."

(EXODUS 32:2-4)

ITEM FOUND: Calf figurine

DISCOVERED: 1990

LOCATION: Ashkelon, Israel (M3)

EXPEDITION: Dr. Lawrence E. Stager

How did God's people end up worshipping a golden calf? To answer this question we must start from the beginning.

Abraham's grandson was Jacob. Jacob had twelve sons by four women. His son Joseph was born to him by his wife Rachel. Joseph was his father's favorite, and this caused all his older brothers to be jealous of him. So, at the first opportune moment, they sold Joseph into slavery in Egypt.

Many years later, after Joseph had risen to power, a severe famine hit the land, and Joseph's brothers were forced to travel to Egypt to seek help. When Joseph saw his brothers, they did not recognize him, so he tested them and eventually revealed his identity to them. He ultimately forgave them for what they had done. Then Joseph invited his entire family: his brothers, their wives and children, as well as his father, Jacob, to leave Canaan and come live under the safety and protection of Pharaoh.

But when that generation died out, a new king came to power who did not know Joseph. He turned the Israelites into slaves, and they remained in Egypt for more than four hundred years until God sent Moses to rescue them.

Moses was born a Hebrew, and in order to save him from Pharaoh's edict of death, his mother placed him in a basket and sent him down the Nile. Pharaoh's daughter found him and raised him in Pharaoh's palace as her own. But when he became a man, he saw one of the Egyptians beating a Hebrew, so Moses killed him.

Fearing for his life, he ran away to Midian and lived there for forty years until God commissioned him from the burning bush (see Exodus 3). Through God's clear instruction and mighty power, Moses was able to lead his people out of slavery in Egypt toward the promised land (see also "Shechem"). Unfortunately, when Moses went up Mount Sinai to receive the Ten Commandments, the people decided to turn from God and fashion their own god out of gold. This handcrafted god was a golden calf made to look like one of the Canaanite gods with which they were familiar.

"Archaeologists excavating an ancient fortress-city have discovered a figurine they believe is the precursor to the biblical Golden Calf that enraged Moses when he descended from Mount Sinai," wrote Jim Rom of the *Guardian*. "The archaeologists said the tiny statue, which predates the biblical Israelites' exodus from Egypt, suggested the Hebrews drew upon an ancient Canaanite tradition when they betrayed Moses by worshiping a pagan deity in his absence."

According to the lead archaeologist of the dig, Dr. Stager, the bronze and silver figurine is from the sixteenth century BC and is four and a half inches high and four and a half inches long. It was discovered in the remains of a pagan temple near the gate of the ancient Canaanite port city of Ashkelon.

GOLIATH'S ARMOR

1 SAMUEL 17

A champion named Goliath, who was from Gath, came out of the Philistine camp. He was over nine feet tall. He had a bronze helmet on his head and wore a coat of scale armor of bronze weighing five thousand shekels; on his legs he wore bronze greaves, and a bronze javelin was slung on his back. His spear shaft was like a weaver's rod, and its iron point weighed six hundred shekels. His shield bearer went ahead of him. (1 SAMUEL 17:4-7)

ITEM FOUND: Picture of armor on a relief

DISCOVERED: 1930s

LOCATION: Medinet Habu, near Thebes, Egypt, along the west bank of the Nile River (M4)

EXPEDITION: Uvo Hölscher

The Israelites' greatest enemies were the Philistines. They had many run-ins and battles with these Sea People. But perhaps the most famous encounter was the tête-à-tête between David and Goliath. Goliath was a strong, professional military man. Perhaps his most recognizable feature was his height, more than nine feet tall. The Israelites were so afraid that they literally shook with fear at the prospect of fighting him.

For forty days Goliath would march up to the battle line and taunt the Israelites, asking for someone to come and fight, but no one dared. As David was the youngest son of his father Jesse, he was not yet old enough to be in the army. His days were occupied with tending sheep. However, on one particular day David went to the battlefield to check on three of his older brothers and heard Goliath's taunts. Immediately, David burned with righteous indignation because Goliath was "defy[ing] the armies of the living God" (vv. 26, 36) So, David approached Goliath the way he was used to approaching an attacking lion or bear—with a simple sling and a stone. On the other side, Goliath was armed to the teeth. As the battle took place during the Bronze Age, it would follow that Goliath would be covered from head to toe in bronze. Even his javelin was made of bronze. Nevertheless, with all of his armor and military experience, Goliath was still no match for God, and as David fought for the Lord, he gained a decisive victory.

According to *Buried History: A Quarterly Journal of Biblical Archaeology*, "The description of Goliath's armor and weapons is perfectly in accord with what we find from archaeological evidence as, for example, the reliefs of Pharaoh Rameses III (c. 1195–1165 BC) on the walls of his great temple at Medinet Habu, Thebes, where his victories over the 'Sea People' (including the Philistines) are portrayed."

This mortuary temple is one of the best preserved and is open to the public.

JAMES, JOSEPH, JESUS

MATTHEW 13

When Jesus had finished these parables, he moved on from there. Coming to his hometown, he began teaching the people in their synagogue, and they were amazed. "Where did this man get this wisdom and these miraculous powers?" they asked. "Isn't this the carpenter's son? Isn't his mother's name Mary, and aren't his brothers James, Joseph, Simon and Judas? Aren't all his sisters with us? Where then did this man get all these things?" And they took offense at him. (MATTHEW 13:53-57)

ITEM FOUND: Ossuary box from circa AD 63 owned by Oded Golan, an Israeli engineer and antiquities collector

DISCOVERED: Unknown

LOCATION: Silwan area in the Kidron Valley, southeast of the Temple Mount near Jerusalem, Israel (M2 and M3)

EXPEDITION: Unknown

Jesus and His life are well documented in the pages of the Bible, but what about Jesus' family? The Scriptures say that Mary was His mother and that her husband was Joseph. The Scriptures also name four of Jesus' brothers and hint that he had at least two sisters. This is not at all surprising, because although Mary was a virgin when she became pregnant with God's Son, Jesus, she married Joseph, and at the appropriate time, would have been expected to bear him children. To the ancient Hebrew, marriage was for the purpose of creating a family. To be unwed was looked down upon. This was because marriage was viewed as an important part of securing the continuation and unity of the nation. Then, as now, in Oriental society, each adult child, through marriage, created a family unit or clan. That clan then became part of the larger tribe, and all the tribes together formed a nation. For this reason it was the wife's supreme duty to have children, and Mary was no exception. As her husband, Joseph had every right to expect Mary to have relations with him (see 1 Corinthians 7:4) and to produce offspring. Furthermore, sons were a blessing to the woman because they were her protectors should anything happen to the patriarch.

The apostle James was one of Jesus' half brothers (see Galatians 1:19). He became a leader in the Jerusalem church. He authored the New Testament book of James and was martyred for his faith in AD 62.

"[Now,] after nearly 2,000 years, historical evidence for the existence of Jesus has come to light literally etched in stone. An inscription has been found on an ancient bone box, called an ossuary that reads 'James, son of Joseph, brother of Jesus.' This container provides the only New Testament–era mention of the central figure of Christianity and is the first-ever archaeological discovery to corroborate biblical references to Jesus," said André Lemaire, doctor of Oriental studies from the University of Paris. Furthermore, Lemaire, a renowned paleographer of the École pratique des hautes études in Paris, authenticated the lettering on the box, which was of a form used only from circa AD 10 to 70.

MAPS

M1
THE SEVEN NATIONS OF CANAAN
DURING THE EXODUS OF JOSHUA'S TIME

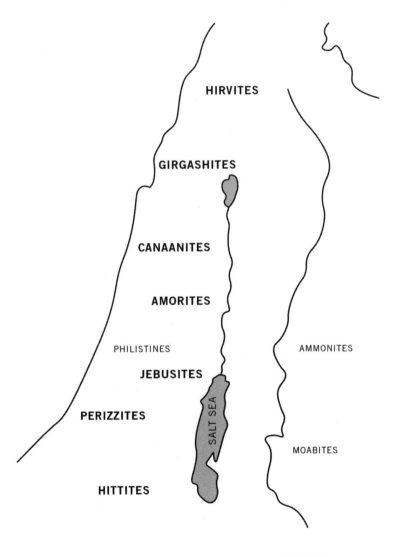

M2
LAND OF THE TWELVE TRIBES AFTER THE EXODUS

M3
MAP OF ISRAEL (THEN AND NOW)

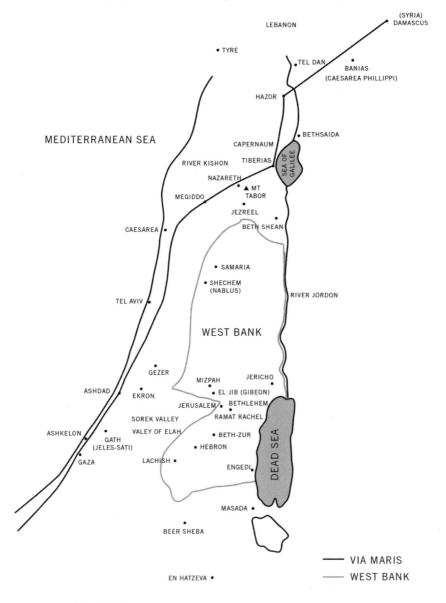

M4

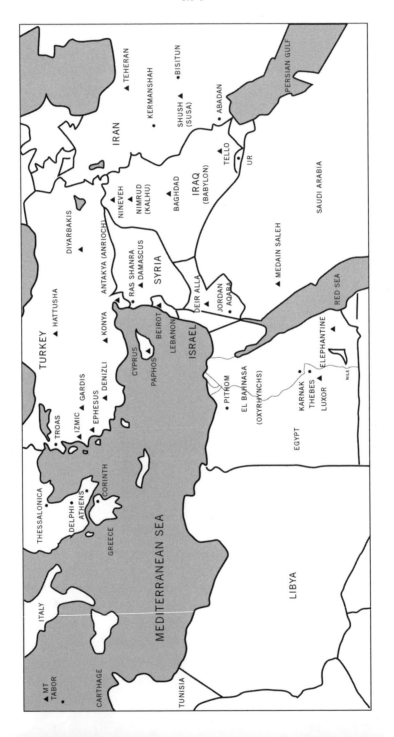

M5
NOAH'S SONS
(GENESIS 10)

JAPHETH	HAM	SHEM
(GEN 10:2-5)	(GEN 10:6-20)	(GEN 10:21-30)
7 SONS	4 SONS	5 SONS
EUROPE AND ASIA	SOUTHWEST ASIA, CANAAN, AFRICA	MIDDLE EAST SHEMITES

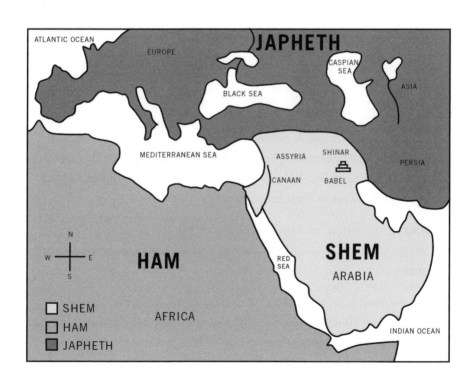

GLOSSARY

ACROPOLIS: the highest elevation of a city

ACHAEMENIDS: members of a Persian dynasty who, under Cyrus II, Cambyses II, Darius I, Xerxes I, and Artaxerxes I, built up a vast empire, conquered Egypt, and attacked Greece. Alexander the Great overthrew it.

AD: *anno Domini*; in the year of our Lord

AGORA: an open market or square in Greek cities, used for public affairs (similar to the Roman forum)

AKKADIAN: a Semitic language spoken in somewhat different dialects by the Babylonians and Assyrians. The name derives from Akkad, a city built by the Babylonian king Sargon of Akkad in about 2300 BC. In the second millennium BC, Akkadian was used as a diplomatic lingua franca throughout the entire Near East.

ANNALS: historical records that relate simply the facts and events of each year, in direct chronological order, without any observations of the annalist

ASHLAR: stones cut in the shape of squares or rectangles that are uniform in size and laid horizontally. Usually they are found laid as a wall in itself or as facing for a rubble wall.

BABYLONIA: the region of south Mesopotamia after the mid-third millennium BC, extending from the Persian Gulf to modern Baghdad. The later Neo-Babylonian Empire, with its capital at Babylon, arose in 612 BC and lasted until the Persian conquest of 539 BC.

BALUSTER: one of the small pillars that support the railing of a staircase or balcony

BALUSTRADE: a row of balusters surmounted by a rail

BASALT: A dark gray to black, dense to fine-grained igneous volcanic rock. Basalt is often found in the mountains of Galilee.

BAS-RELIEF: A three-dimensional sculpture in which the figures project slightly from the background

BC: Before Christ

BCE: Before the Common Era; used by some instead of *BC* to eliminate any reference to Christ.

BULLA (PL., BULLAE): a small lump of clay used in antiquity to seal the strings around documents, and impressed with the name of the sender

CE: Common Era; used instead of *AD, Anno Domini,* or *In the year of our Lord,* by those wishing to eliminate any reference to Christ

CUNEIFORM: the earliest known system of writing, consisting of triangular markings pressed on a clay tablet; developed by the Sumerians in about 3000 BC

CYLINDER SEAL: a cylinder, usually of stone, carved with figures, designs, or writing

DAUB: any soft, sticky material for coating an object

DUNAM: A Greek measurement equating to one-fourth acre

HYKSOS: Asian invaders who ruled Egypt between the thirteenth- and seventeenth-century dynasties

HYPOCORISTICON: a name composed of a compressed sentence

MESOPOTAMIA: literally the land between the Tigris and Euphrates rivers, stretching from the Persian Gulf to the foothills of southeastern Anatolia, a region now mostly covered by Iraq and Iran

MINIMALIST: a person that believes the Bible cannot be considered reliable evidence for what happened in ancient Israel

NIHILIST: someone who believes life is meaningless and rejects all religious and moral principles

OSTRACA: pieces of clay with writing on them (sing., ostracon). The word comes from the Greek *ostrakon*, meaning "shell, sherd." Most ostraca were written on with ink, but some were incised with a sharp instrument. School lessons, short letters, receipts, and other administrative documents were written on these clay sherds because they were cheap and plentiful.

PAPYRUS: a kind of paper made from reeds growing in the Nile River. This material, which was made only in Egypt, had to be imported and was very expensive to use. Eventually the Greeks modified the name to *papure*, which is where we get the word *paper*.

PARCHMENT: treated animal skins used in the ancient Near East and Egypt to write on

PESTLE: A blunt-ended implement used for reducing hard substances to powder by pounding them in a mortar

POTSHERDS: broken pieces of ceramic pottery

SCARABOID: a small seal that was used to make an impression in clay (sometimes wax)

SEPULCHER: a tomb, esp. one cut in rock

SOUK: (in Arab countries) a market

STRATUM: 1: a layer of soil containing artifacts and debris representing a particular time and culture at a site (pl., strata); 2: the combination of all loci belonging to one construction, habitation, and destruction cycle representing one historical and cultural period of habitation at one site. These are usually distinguished from one another by differences in soil makeup, artifacts, and architecture.

SUMER: the first major civilization in Mesopotamia, which included the city-states of Eridu, Ur, Nippur, and Uruk (the last, according to a king list, was ruled by Gilgamesh around 2700 BC)

SUMERIAN: a language of southern Mesopotamia that ceased to be spoken after about 2000 BC.

SUMERIAN: a native of Sumer, thought to be perhaps the first civilization (c. 3500–1600 BC). Sumerian people originally migrated from the Armenian region of the Black and Caspian Sea area. They created the world's earliest known writing system toward the end of the fourth millennium BC, as well as some of the world's earliest literature in the third millennium BC.

TEL: the Hebrew word (*tell* in Arabic) used to refer to a mound of earth made by the repeated destruction and rebuilding of ancient cities and villages on that same site

ACKNOWLEDGMENTS

First and foremost, I would like to thank my Lord and Savior, Jesus Christ, for all He has done for me. This book could *never* have been possible without Him. After all, it was He who planted the desire in my heart to go to Israel and who gave me the courage to go ahead with the travel plans even while the country was in turmoil. He protected and blessed us every step of the way, and it was He who opened my eyes to the evidences found within these pages. Without my Lord this book would never have been conceived, much less completed, and for this I give Him full praise and glory!

I would also like to thank my husband and friend, David P. Brody, who has been my number one fan throughout this entire project. He has spent countless and tireless hours researching and was an endless source of ideas and insight. He believed in this endeavor and he believes in me. But most of all he prayed for me and encouraged me when I felt overwhelmed, and he helped me to see the finish line.

I would like to thank my three children, Drew, Lance, and Arielle, who cheered me on and who were genuinely interested in this idea and its success. XOXO

To my father, Capt. Conrad J. Bassett, who was a gentle, giving man: I thank him for my education and the means to travel around the world. But most of all for the many hours we enjoyed walking through the park on the way home from school.

To my aunt Lissia E. Rodriguez: Thank you for holding down the fort so I could work on the book and for all the delicious meals you made.

To Kristen Brody, whose phone calls, words of encouragement, and cheers really helped push me through.

A special thanks to Pastor Lon Solomon, who prayerfully toured us around Israel and whose teachings have always been interesting, informative, inspirational, and blessed. Thank you, also, for writing such a wonderful foreword.

Thanks to all my professors at Capital Bible Seminary for their excellent teaching, dedication to students, and love of the Word. And a special thanks to Drs. Beall and Yates for making my years in seminary a time of growth as a Christian and for your support of my book.

Thanks to everyone who helped me pick the title of this book by responding to my informal e-mail poll. These include: Robin Bassett, René Bassett, Lissia Rodriguez, Cassie Rosenberg, Chris and Gina Ruiz, Mr. and Mrs. C. Bassett, Dani Gonzalez, Kim Bouchard, Carmen and John Thigpen, Brandon Estela, David Bango, Cathi Miller, Melanie Doyle, Mary Macnamara, Anastasia Portnoy, and Donna Boyajy.

SOURCES

AHAZ
Birmingham Post & Mail Ltd., "Fingerprint Relic from Biblical King," January 2, 1998, cached at http://www.thefreelibrary.com/fingerprint relic from biblical king.-a060861147.

Robert Deutsch, *Messages from the Past: Hebrew Bullae from the Time of Isaiah through the Destruction of the First Temple* (Tel Aviv: Archaeological Center Publications, 1999), 61.

AMMONITES
Larry G. Herr, "What Ever Happened to the Ammonites?" *Biblical Archeology Review*, November/December 1993, 30.

BELSHAZZAR
Raymond Philip Dougherty, *Nabonidus and Belshazzar: A Study of the Closing Events of the Neo-Babylonian Empire* (New Haven, CT: Yale University Press, 1929), 192, 196, 197, 200.

Clyde E. Fant and Mitchell Glenn Reddish, *Lost Treasures of the Bible: Understanding the Bible through Archaeological Artifacts in World Museums* (Grand Rapids: Eerdmans, 2008), 233.

Ferrell Jenkins, "The Big Three: Nabonidus, Belshazzar and Daniel," *Ferrell's Travel Blog*, February 24, 2012, http://ferrelljenkins.wordpress.com/2012/02/24/the-big-three-nabonidus-belshazzar-and-daniel/.

CAIAPHAS
Jeffery L. Sheler, "Extraordinary Insights from Archaeology and History," *U.S. News & World Report*, October 25, 1999, 58–59.

CYRUS KING OF PERSIA
HLB, "The Cyrus Cylinder," Intriguing History, accessed April 20, 2017, http://www.intriguing-history.com/cyrus-cylinder/.

Amélie Kuhrt, *The Ancient Near East c. 3000–330 BC*, vol. 1 (Abingdon, UK: Psychology Press, 1995), 647.

James Orr, "Cyrus," in *International Standard Bible Encyclopedia*, StudyLight.org, accessed April 20, 2017, http://www.studylight.org/encyclopedias/isb/view.cgi?n=2479&search=cyrus#cyrus.

Hershel Shanks, *Jerusalem: An Archaeological Biography* (New York: Random House, 1995), 119.

DAVID
Jeffery L. Sheler, "Extraordinary Insights from Archaeology and History," *U.S. News and World Report*, October 25, 1999, 50, 52.

EDOMITES
Itzhaq Beit-Arieh, "Edomites Advance into Judah: Israelite Defensive Fortresses Inadequate," *Biblical Archaeology Review*, November/December 1996, 30–31.

Gary D. Pratico, "Nelson Glueck's 1938–1940 Excavations at Tell El-Kheleifeh: A Reappraisal," *Biblical Archeology*, January 1, 1985, http://www.bible.ca/archeology/bible-archeology-exodus-kadesh-barnea-ezion-geber-nelson-gluecks-1938-1940-excavations-tell-el-kheleifeh-reappraisal-gary-pratico-1985ad.htm.

GEDALIAH
Ernest G. Wright, "Some Personal Seals of Judean Royal Officials," *Biblical Archeologist* 1, no. 2 (1938): 11.

GEMARIAH
Christine Temin, "The City of David Brings an Ancient Civilization Back to Life," *Boston Globe*, November 10, 1991, A2.

HITTITES
Cullen Murphy, "Huiswants Es," *Atlantic*, August 1, 1992, 19.
Billie Jean Collins, *The Hittites and Their World*, Archaeology and Biblical Studies (Atlanta: Society of Biblical Literature, 2007), 107.

JEROBOAM II
David Ussishkin, "Gate 1567 at Megiddo and the Seal of Shema, Servant of Jeroboam," in *Scripture and Other Artifacts: Essays on the Bible and Archaeology in Honor of Philip J. King*, ed. Michael D. Coogan, J. Cheryl Exum, and Lawrence E. Stager (Louisville: Westminster John Knox Press, 1994), 419–20.

KING HEROD THE GREAT
Hilary Appelman, "Archaeologists Unearth Wine Jug Used by King Herod," AP News Archive, July 8, 1996, http://www.apnewsarchive.com/1996/Archaeologists-Unearth-Wine-Jug-Used-By-King-Herod/id-90395cb8b65d3a03f0f695d5b6ccb327.

KING HEROD AGRIPPA I
Tim Dowley, *Discovering the Bible: Archaeologists Look at Scripture* (Basingstoke, UK: Marshall Pickering, 1986), 72–73.

KING HEROD AGRIPPA II
John C. H. Laughlin, *Fifty Major Cities of the Bible* (New York: Routledge, 2006), 83.

NEBUCHADNEZZAR
"Ancient Babylonia—The Babylonian Chronicles," Bible History Online, accessed April 20, 2017, http://www.bible-history.com/babylonia/BabyloniaThe_Babylonian_Chronicle00000053.htm.
Jeffery L. Sheler, *Is the Bible True? How Modern Debates and Discoveries Affirm the Essence of the Scriptures* (San Francisco: HarperSanFrancisco/Zondervan, 1999), 107.

PHILISTINES
Jeffery L. Sheler, "Extraordinary Insights from Archaeology and History," U.S. News and World Report (October 25, 1999), 56–58.
James Orr, "Philistines," International Standard Bible Encyclopedia, StudyLight.org, Online: http://www.studylight.org/enc/isb/view.cgi?n=6834.
Michael G. Hasel, "New Discoveries Among the Philistines: Archaeological and Textual Considerations," Journal of the Adventist Theological Society 9/1-2 (1998), 58.

PONTIUS PILATE
Jeffery L. Sheler, "Extraordinary Insights from Archaeology and History," *U.S. News & World Report*, October 25, 1999, 59.

SENNACHERIB
The British Museum, "Sennacherib the Assyrian Lays Siege to Jerusalem," Google Arts & Culture, accessed April 20, 2017, https://www.google.com/culturalinstitute/beta/asset/sennacherib-the-assyrian-lays-siege-to-jerusalem/jQGyPHzdLoU8lw.

Ronald Harker and Martin Simmons, *Digging Up the Bible Lands* (New York: Random House Childrens Books, 1973), 44–45.

TIGLATH-PILESER (PUL)
James B. Pritchard, Archaeology and the Old Testament (Princeton, NY: Princeton University Press, 1958), 148–150.

UZZIAH
Ernest G. Wright, "A Gravestone of Uzziah, King of Judah," *Biblical Archeologist* 1, no. 2 (1938): 8–9.

ANTIOCH
Encyclopedia Britannica, s.v. "Antioch," accessed October 7, 2014, https://www.britannica.com/place/Antioch-modern-and-ancient-city-south-central-Turkey.

Werner Keller, *The Bible as History: Archaeology Confirms the Book of Books* (London: Hodder and Stoughton, 1974), 364.

BETHEL
William G. Dever and Shalom M. Paul, eds., *Biblical Archaeology* (Jerusalem: Keter, 1973), 70.

BETHSAIDA
Rami Arav, Richard A. Freund, and John F. Shroder Jr., "Bethsaida Rediscovered," *Biblical Archaeology Review* 26, no. 1 (January/February 2000): 45.

BETH SHEMESH
Shlomo Bunimovitz and Zvi Lederman, "Beth Shemesh Culture Conflict on Judah's Frontier," *Biblical Archaeology Review* 23, no. 1 (January/February 1997): 43.

CAESAREA PHILIPPI
Mary Rourke, "In the Beginning," *Los Angeles Times*, October 6, 1999, E1, E4, http://articles.latimes.com/1999/oct/06/news/cl-19202.

CANAAN
William Foxwell Albright, *Recent Discoveries in Bible Lands: A Sketch* (New York: Funk & Wagnalls, 1936), 4.

T. C. Mitchell, *Biblical Archaeology: Documents from the British Museum* (Cambridge, UK: Cambridge University Press, 1988), 41.

CAPERNAUM
Jeffery L. Sheler, *Is the Bible True?: How Modern Debates and Discoveries Affirm the Essence of the Scriptures* (San Francisco: HarperSanFrancisco/Zondervan, 1999), 117.

WebBible Encyclopedia, s.v. "Capernaum," accessed August 2013, http://christiananswers.net/dictionary/capernaum.html.

EN GEDI
"Ein Gedi Walking: Early History of Ein Gedi," DeadSea.com, accessed April 21, 2017, http://www.deadsea.com/explore/outdoors-recreation/nature-hiking/ein-gedi-walking/.

Israel Ministry of Foreign Affairs, "Ein Gedi—An Ancient Oasis Settlement," November 23, 1999, http://www.mfa.gov.il/mfa/israelexperience/history/pages/ein gedi - an ancient oasis settlement.aspx.

Israel Nature and Parks Authority, "En Gedi Nature Reserve," Parks.org, accessed April 21, 2017, http://www.parks.org.il/sites/English/ParksAndReserves/engedi/Pages/default.aspx.

Rotem (webmaster), "Ein Gedi," BibleWalks.com, updated June 13, 2013, http://www.biblewalks.com/Sites/EinGedi.html.

GATH

Calev Ben-David, "Tell It in Gath," *Jerusalem Post*, August 10, 2001, 11.

Noah Wiener, "Philistine and Israelite Religion at Tell es-Safi/Gath," Bible History Daily, August 1, 2014, http://www.biblicalarchaeology.org/daily/ancient-cultures/ancient-israel/philistine-and-israelite-religion-at-tell-es-safigath/.

GIBEAH

Azriel Louis Eisenberg, and Dov Peretz Elkins, *Treasures from the Dust* (New York: Abelard-Schuman, 1972), 41, 42, 44.

HAZOR

Biblical Archaeological Society, "Tel Hazor," Find a Dig, accessed April 21, 2017, http://digs.bib-arch.org/digs/tel-hazor.asp.

Ross Dunn, "Excavated Tablets Provide Clue to Canaan Treasures," *Times of London*, July 31, 1996, 11.

HEBRON

Deborah Horan, "Relics from Abraham's Time Found in Hebron/Find Indicates Area Was Site of Biblical City," *Houston Chronicle*, October 1, 2001, 25A.

Matthew Kalman, "Israeli Dig Finds Traces of Lost City of Abraham," *Sunday Times* (London), July 4, 1999, http://matthewkalman.blogspot.com/1999_07_01_archive.html.

MEGIDDO

LaMar C. Berrett and D. Kelly Ogden, *Discovering the World of the Bible* (Provo: Young House, 1973), 106.

Shalom M. Paul, *Biblical Archaeology*, ed. William G. Dever (Jerusalem: Keter, 1973), 138–39.

NAZARETH

Michael Avi-Yonah, "A List of Priestly Courses from Caesarea," *Israel Exploration Journal* 12, no. 2 (1962): 137–39.

Time-Life Editors, *The Holy Land* (Alexandria, VA: Time-Life Books, 1992), 124–25.

NINEVEH

Gordon G. Garner, *Royal Cities of Assyria: Archaeology, the Bible, and the Capitals of Ancient Assyria* (Melbourne: Australian Institute of Archaeology, 1981), 100, 101, 112, 114.

SAMARIA

Willis J. Beecher, "The Date of the Downfall of Samaria," *Journal of Biblical Literature* 11, no. 2 (1892): 211–13.

Kathleen M. Kenyon, *Archaeology in the Holy Land* (London: E. Benn, 1979), 258–63.

SHECHEM

LaMoine F. DeVries, *Cities of the Biblical World* (Peabody, MA: Hendrickson, 1997), 231, 234.

SUSA

Avraham Negev, *Archaeological Encyclopedia of the Holy Land* (New York: Continuum, 2001), 469–70.

James Orr, *International Standard Bible Encyclopedia*, s.v. "Shushan," accessed April 21, 2017, http://www.studylight.org/enc/isb/view.cgi?n=8049.

"The World's 20 Oldest Cities," *Telegraph*, June 14, 2016, http://www.telegraph.co.uk/travel/destinations/middleeast/11105676/The-worlds-20-oldest-cities.html?frame=3043210.

TYRE

R. B. Bement, *Tyre; the History of Phoenicia, Palestine and Syria, and the Final Captivity of Israel and Judah by the Assyrians* (N.p.: Ulan Press, 2012), 47.

Sara Japhet, "In Search of Ancient Israel: Revision at All Costs," *The Jewish Past Revisited: Reflections on Modern Jewish Historians*, ed. David N. Myers (New Haven, CT: Yale University Press, 1998), 225.

MiddleEast.com, "Countries: Tyre," accessed November 4, 2014, http://www.middleeast.com/tyre.htm.

UR OF THE CHALDEANS
Werner Keller, *The Bible as History* (New York: Barnes and Noble Books, 1995), 40.

AHAB'S HOUSE OF IVORY
Michael Avi-Yonah, *A History of Israel and the Holy Land* (New York and London: Continuum, 2005), 88.

BOAT
The Oxford Encyclopedia of Near Eastern Archaeology, ed E. M. Meyers (New York: Oxford University Press, 1997), s.v. "Galilee Boat," by Shelley Wachsmann, 2:377.

DRACHMA
Joseph P. Free and Howard F. Vos, *Archaeology and Bible History* (Grand Rapids: Zondervan, 1992), 213.

HEZEKIAH'S RESERVOIR
David L. Chandler, "Geologist Gets to Bottom of Biblical Mystery," *Boston Globe*, August 13, 2001, 25–26.

Hershel Shanks, *Jerusalem: An Archaeological Biography* (New York: Random House, 1995), 80.

HEZEKIAH'S TUNNEL
Hebrew University of Jerusalem, "Dating of King Hezekiah's Tunnel Verified by Scientists," EurekAlert!, September 10, 2003, http://www.eurekalert.org/pub_releases/2003-09/huoj-dok090903.php.

Émile Puech, "L'inscription du Tunnel de Siloé," *Revue Biblique* 81 (1974): 196–214.

HIGH PLACE
Richard N. Ostling, "Insights from Israel's Longest-Running Archaeological Dig," *Daily Courier*, January 15, 1999, 8B.

HORNS OF THE ALTAR
Yohanan Aharoni, "The Horned Altar at Beer-Sheba," *Biblical Archaeologist* 37 (March 1974): 2–6.

Gaalyahu Cornfeld, *Archaeology of the Bible: Book by Book* (New York: Harper & Row, 1976), 119–20.

International Standard Bible Encyclopedia, s.v. "Horns of the Altar," accessed April 24, 2017, http://www.studylight.org/encyclopedias/isb/view.cgi?n=4398.

JEHOIAKIM'S PALACE
Leila Leah Bronner, *Biblical Personalities and Archaeology* (Jerusalem: Keter, 1974), 173–75.

Benjamin Lau, "Portion of the Week in a Land Not Sown," Haaretz, July 25, 2008, http://www.haaretz.com/portion-of-the-week-in-a-land-not-sown-1.250405.

JEZREEL PALACE
William G. Dever, *What Did the Biblical Writers Know, and When Did They Know It?: What Archaeology Can Tell Us about the Reality of Ancient Israel* (Grand Rapids, MI: Eerdmans Publishing, 2001), 239–241.

International Standard Bible Encyclopedia, "Ahab: no. 4," StudyLight.org, accessed April 24, 2017, http://www.studylight.org/encyclopedias/isb/view.cgi?n=291&search=Ahab#Ahab.

Matthew Henry, "1 Kings 21:1-4," *Matthew Henry's Commentary on the Whole Bible: New Modern Edition*, electronic database, 1991, Hendrickson Publishers.

PETER'S HOUSE

Gerusalemme San Salvatore Convento Francescano St. Saviour's Monastery, "Two Archaeologists at the Doors of Peter's House," Sanctuary Capernaum, accessed April 24, 2017, http://www.capernaum.custodia.org/default.asp?id=5380.

Jeffery L. Sheler, *Is the Bible True?: How Modern Debates and Discoveries Affirm the Essence of the Scriptures* (San Francisco: HarperSanFrancisco/Zondervan, 1999), 118.

PIM

Azriel Louis Eisenberg and Dov Peretz Elkins, *Treasures from the Dust* (New York: Abelard-Schuman, 1972), 52–55.

POMEGRANATE

David Briggs, "Testaments: Archaeological Discoveries Provide Biblical Evidence," *Stevens Point Journal*, December 8, 1993, 8.

Matthew Henry, *Matthew Henry's Commentary on the Whole Bible: New Modern Edition* (1991), electronic database.

James Orr, "Pomegranate" in *International Standard Bible Encyclopedia*, StudyLight.org, accessed April 20, 2017, http://www.studylight.org/encyclopedia/isb/view.cgi?n=6951&search=pomegranate#pomegranate.

POOL OF BETHESDA

"Biblical Archaeology: Good Grounds for Faith," *U.S. Catholic* 57, no. 7 (July 1, 1994): 18.

Pat McCarthy, "Pools of Bethesda," seetheholyland.net, accessed April 24, 2017, http://www.seetheholyland.net/pools-of-bethesda/.

POOL OF GIBEON

James Orr, s.v. "Gibeon," *International Standard Bible*, StudyLight.org accessed April 20, 2017, http://www.studylight.org/encyclopedias/isb/view.cgi?n=3762.

Bryant Wood, "Scholars Speak Out," Biblical Archaeology Review 21:3 (May-June 1995), 33.

POOL OF SILOAM

Associated Press, "Archaeologists Identify Traces of 'Miracle' Pool," NBCNews.com, December 23, 2004, http://www.nbcnews.com/id/6750670#.WP4hg9LyuUk

RACHEL'S TOMB

Dovid Rossoff, "Tomb of Rachel," *Jewish Magazine*, October 1997, http://www.jewishmag.com/2mag/israel/israel.htm.

Travel Palestine, "Bethlehem Attractions: Rachel's Tomb," accessed April 24, 2017, http://travel-palestine.ps/?s=rachel's tomb.

TEMPLE OF ARTEMIS

Chris Scarre, *London Times* Newspapers Limited, August 17, 1991, 17.

TEMPLE OF THE ASHTORETHS

Alan Rowe, "Discovery of the Temple of Ashteroth: Report of the Expedition to Palestine," *Museum Journal* 16 (1925): 309, 311.

THEATER OF EPHESUS

John Elder, *Prophets, Idols and Diggers: Scientific Proof of Bible History* (Indianapolis: Bobbs-Merrill, 1960), 220.

WALLS OF JERICHO

John Garstang, "Jericho and the Biblical Story," in *Wonders of the Past*, ed. J. A. Hammerton, 2 vols. (New York: Wise, 1937), 2:1222.

Bryant G. Wood, "Did the Israelites Conquer Jericho? A New Look at the Archaeological Evidence," Associates for Biblical Research website, May 1, 2008, http://www.biblearchaeology.org/post/2008/05/did-the-israelites-conquer-jericho-a-new-look-at-the-archaeological-evidence.aspx#Article.

BAAL WORSHIP
Roberta L. Harris, *The World of the Bible* (New York: Thames and Hudson, 1995), 52–53.

BRICK WITHOUT STRAW
Jasper A. Huffman, *Voices from Rocks and Dust Heaps of Bible Lands* (Marion, IN: Standard Press, 1928), 41–42.

CAMEL
Brian Hesse, "Animal Husbandry and Human Diet in the Ancient Near East," in *Civilizations of the Near East*, ed. J. M. Sasson, 2 vols. (New York: Charles Scribner's Sons, 1995), 1:217.
K. A. Kitchen, *Ancient Orient and Old Testament* (Chicago: Inter-Varsity Press, 1966), 79–80.
Rabbi Dovid Lichtman, "Archaeology and the Bible—Part 2: Is There Archaeological Evidence That Supports the Bible?" aish.com, accessed April 25, 2017, http://www.aish.com/ci/sam/48939077.html.
Chris Scarre, *Smithsonian Timelines of the Ancient World* (London: DK Adult, 1993), 176.

CHILD SACRIFICE
Richard David Barnett, *Illustrations of Old Testament History* (London: British Museum Publications, 1966), 37–38.

DAVID SLAYS GOLIATH
Buried History: A Quarterly Journal of Biblical Archaeology 2, no. 1 (1965): 3.

DEATH BY CRUCIFIXION
William D. Edwards, Wesley J. Gabel, and Floyd E. Hosmer, "Scourging and Crucifixion in Roman Tradition," Truth of God, accessed April 25, 2017, http://cbcg.org/scourging_crucifixion.htm.
Encyclopedia Britannica, s.v. "Crucifixion," accessed April 25, 2017, http://www.britannica.com/EBchecked/topic/144583/crucifixion.
Vassilios Tzaferis, "Crucifixion—The Archaeological Evidence," *Biblical Archaeology Review*, January/February 1985, 44–53.

THE BURNING OF HAZOR
Biblical Archaeology Society, "Tel Hazor: The Head of All Those Kingdoms," Find a Dig, accessed April 25, 2017, http://digs.bib-arch.org/digs/tel-hazor.asp.
David Briggs, "Digs Uncover Biblical Support," *Augusta Chronicle*, December 14, 1996, B1–2, http://old.chronicle.augusta.com/stories/1996/12/14/met_201272.shtml.

GOLDEN CALF
Jim Rom, "Biblical Treasure May Be Forerunner of the Golden Calf," *Guardian*, July 26, 1990, 11.

GOLIATH'S ARMOR
Buried History: A Quarterly Journal of Biblical Archaeology 2, no. 1 (1965): 6.

JAMES, JOSEPH, JESUS
Andre Lemaire, "Burial Box of James the Brother of Jesus," *Biblical Archaeology Review*, November/December 2002, 24–33.
James Orr, "Marriage," in *International Standard Bible Encyclopedia*, StudyLight.org, accessed April 25, 2017, http://www.studylight.org/enc/isb/view.cgi?n=5765.

ABOUT THE AUTHOR

Lisette Bassett-Brody graduated summa cum laude in 2013 from Capital Bible Seminary with a master's degree in biblical studies. In 1987, she earned a BA from Syracuse University in modern foreign languages. Her writing achievements include published articles for *Bible and Spade* magazine and for a Colorado Springs newspaper called the *Briargate Edition*. She has been a part of the Community Bible Study (CBS) program since 1995 and has been a core leader. Lisette married her husband, David, in 1988, and they have three children. They live in Maryland.

PHOTO CREDITS

INDEX

Jesus, archaeological evidence for the existence of, 222–23

Jesus Boat, 133–35

Jewish Past Revisited: Reflections on Modern Jewish Historians, The (Japhet), 125

Jezebel (queen), 131–32, 155–56

Jezreel palace, 154–56

Joseph (father of Jesus), archaeological evidence for the existence of, 221–23

Joshua (leader of Israel), 94, 96, 98, 101, 103, 104, 124, 188–89, 198, 199

K

Keller, Werner, 68, 128

Kelso, J. L., 70

Kenyon, Dame Kathleen, 115, 189

Koldewey, Robert, 48–49

Kuyunjik, Iraq, 57, 111–12. *See* Nineveh

L

Lachish, Israel, 27, 28

Laughlin, John C. H., 46

Layard, Austen Henry, 60, 61, 110

Lederman, Zvi, 77

Lemaire, André, 4, 223

Lichtman, Dovid, 203

limestone slab (photo), 51

Lion Hunt Reliefs, 112

Loffreda, Stanislao, 158, 159

Loftus, William Kenneth, 120

Lost Treasures of the Bible (Fant and Reddish), 11

Lufan, Moshe and Yuval, 135

M

Macalister, R.A.S., 162

Mackenzie, Duncan, 77

Maeir, Aren, 91, 92

Makridi Bey, Theodore, 33

Masada, Israel, 39, 40

Mayo Clinic, 212–13

Mazar, Benjamin, 88

Medinet Habu, 51, 219, 220

Medo-Persian Empire, 11

Megiddo, 36, 98, 102–4, 150

Mesopotamia, 117, 118, 128, 177, 203, 231, 232, 233

Messages from the Past (Deutsch), 4

Montefiore, Sir Moses, 177

mosaic floors, 40, 68, 80

Moses (patriarch), 27, 30, 83, 100–101, 107, 165, 171, 188, 196, 199, 202, 216–17

Mosul, Iraq, 60, 110. *See also* Nineveh

Museum Journal, 183

Muslims, 101, 107, 117, 177

N

Nablus (West Bank). *See* Shechem

Nabonidus, 11

nations deriving from the sons of Noah, 229

Naville, Edouard, 196, 197

Nazareth, 40, 85, 105–8

Nebuchadnezzar II (king), 10, 11, 17, 28, 31, 47–49, 119, 124, 152

Negev, Avraham, 121

Negev, Israel, 149, 201

Neo-Babylonian Empire, 10, 17, 48, 231

Netzer, Ehud, 39, 40

Nimrud (near present-day Mosul), 60, 61

Nineveh, 57–58, 109–12